BENNY BENION
The Dallas Vigilantes and Texas Hold'em Poker

Other Books in Print
By Jim Gatewood

THE JFK ASSASSINATION A MAFIA HIT

SHERIFF BILL DECKER A TEXAS LEGEND

CAPTAIN WILL FRITZ AND THE DALLAS MAFIA

J. FRANK NORRIS – TOP O' HILL CASINO – LEW
JENKINS AND THE TEXAS OIL RICH

SLATS RODGERS AND THE LOVE FIELD LUNATICS

BONNIE AND CLYDE'S BABY DAUGHTER

To order from the website: WWW.DCARB.COM
To order by phone: (972) 278 5763

BENNY BINION – THE DALLAS VIGILANTES AND

TEXAS HOLDEM POKER

STORIES FROM THE STREETS OF DALLAS

FIRST EDITION

JIM GATEWOOD

Mullaney Corporation

Library of Congress Control Number: 2012918540
ISBN: Hardcover   978-1-4797-2802-2
                 Softcover   978-1-4797-2801-5
                 Ebook   978-1-4797-2803-9

To order additional copies of this book, contact:
Xlibris Corporation
1-888-795-4274
www.Xlibris.com
Orders@Xlibris.com

To James Virgil Counts 6935 E. 15 #125
Tulsa Oklahoma 7412-7406

An elderly man whose body was ravaged by the disease of time and was shutting down had his daughter drive him to see me from her home in Oklahoma. He had heard that I was writing a book about his friend and Leavenworth prison cell mate Benny Binion.

His daughter by his side, it was difficult for him to move as he entered my office. "Virg" told me he was first incarcerated at the age of thirteen in Gatesville Texas Reformatory. He had spent twenty-seven years of his life in prison behind bars.

Known in the trade as a knob knocker, Mr. Counts was a safecracker. His soft brown eyes grew bright as he told stories of his friend and cell mate.

I have James Virgil Counts to thank for even further insight and stories of the Dallas gambler Benny Binion.

Many thanks to Mona Driskill, grammatical coach for her tireless effort spent proofreading.

CONTENTS

PROLOGUE

BEN LESTER BINION was the first child born to Lonnie Lee Binion and his wife, Alma Willie Binion. He suffered five cases of pneumonia before he was two but he survived. A second child, Dorothy, was born, then later a brother, Jack.

The family cotton plantation, Benny Binion's birthplace, is located about sixty miles north of Dallas. At the turn of the century, Pilot Grove was the thriving rural community.

During the Civil War, Pilot Grove was used by Quantrell and his men, as well as wandering soldiers from Missouri and deserters from both sides who preyed on the locals. Bitter feuds and vendettas developed as the carpetbaggers and the rabble formed gangs and fought for political control of the area. A polarization of the territory solidified with the return of a dashing young captain of the Confederate cavalry, Robert J. Lee. He served with one of the most dreaded Southern cavalry generals of the war Nathan Bedford Forrest.

Benny grew up with families that were kin to the dashing Robert J. Lee. He listened at the knee of "Bobby" Lee's descendants to the stories of conspiracy, bribes, fighting, killings, bloodshed, and treachery. His childhood games with his friends emulated the stories, and Captain Bobby Lee was always the hero.

Gambling was an intricate part of the Pilot Grove society with the center of activity, the Pilot Grove mule barn. The men gambled with cards, dominoes, dice, cockfights, horse races, bare knuckle fights, and anything with an unknown element. Young Benny Binion spent more time at the mule barn than he did in school.

BENNY'S EIGHTY-THIRD BIRTHDAY

Novemeber 30, 1987, there was an amazing birthday party in Las Vegas, a spectacular over-the-top party even for Sin City. Eighteen thousand guests attended the eighty-third birthday of the godfather of Las Vegas, Benny Binion.

The entertainers are world-famous country and Western singers Willie Nelson and Hank Williams Jr. A toast is proposed by casino mogul Steve Wynn and a four-tier birthday cake is wheeled onto the stage as all eyes turn to the portly eighty-three-year-old man in the white Stetson sitting in a rocking chair at the center of the stage and a chant begins, *"Benny! Benny! Benny!"* and a fourteen-foot bronze statue of Benny on horseback is unveiled.

This is the crowning moment of Benny Binion's life, tonight he is the star—good old Benny, Benny the family man, Benny the philanthropist, Benny the entrepreneur, Benny the small-time gambler's protector and the poker players' patron saint, Benny the founder of both the World Series of Poker and the game's hall of fame, Benny who, Steve Wynn now tells the cheering crowd, is *"the greatest guy we ever met!"* The old man in the rocking chair dozed.

The name of an Irish indentured prisoner, Zeph Binion, appears on the British manifest of the sailing ship *Ann* that sailed from England November 16, 1732. Binion was indentured for twelve years. He and two hundred twenty-one men, women, and a few children spent two weary months in a small and smelly ship that wallowed in a strange sea as it made its way to the new world.

James Oglethorpe, founder of the colony of Georgia, had petitioned King George of England to release to him from debtor's prison, and into indentured slavery, unfortunate debtors that had run upon hard times and who were otherwise sound, solid, and respectable. The men that were selected were put immediately into military training as soldiers were needed for Oglethorpe's and the British Empire's plans for the new world.

In the afternoons, you could see the men drilling in front of Buckingham Palace. Sergeants of the Royal Guard instructed them in the manual of arms.

The English sailing ship *Ann* reached Charleston, South Carolina, on January 13, 1733, then after a few days' rest, sailed on to Georgia and into the Savannah River, where they dropped anchor eighteen miles upstream (named after the local Savannah Indian tribe). At a point where the high bluffs met the river on the south side, the colonists made camp. These same high bluffs offered excellent protection for a community against the high waters of the spring floods, and a natural harbor would later develop into a major seaport for the export of cotton and the import of farming tools.

If the indentured slave agreed to remain four years after completing his service satisfactorily, he would be assigned twenty-five acres that could be increased to fifty should they commit to become permanent inhabitants of the colony. The former slave's master was required to furnish him with a mule, farming implements, and the first year's seed. Fifty acres of the rich Georgia soil was sufficient to produce a modest fortune depending on a good cotton crop.

Georgia was the last and the farthermost south of the original colonies, creating a frontier buffer between the English and the Spanish Empire in Florida. It would be only a short thirty-three years later that Georgia would become involved in the Revolutionary War against England.

Fast-forward your historical calendar to May 6, 1864. The Union Army under General William T. Sherman is poised with one hundred thousand troops in northern Georgia. Sherman has boasted to Grant that he will make the Southern women wail for food for their starving children. He then burned a path through Georgia to the sea and turned north to punish South Carolina.

General Grant showed no compassion as Georgia and South Carolina were considered the main troublemakers and the very seat of the Confederate conspiracy refusing to pay taxes on cotton and determined to secede from the Union. The Binion family's cotton plantation was located "Ground Zero," directly in the path of Sherman's terrible destruction just north of Atlanta in Barstove County. They were victims of General Sherman's rape of Georgia.

Thomas Noel Binion, at the age of forty-two (patriarch of the Texas branch of the Binion family), and his wife, Pauline, were burned out by Sherman. Bringing their aged mother and father, twin brothers William and Orval, and another younger brother James with them, the Binion family traveled from Barstove County, Georgia, with all their worldly possessions in wagons drawn by mules. It was a trip of one thousand plus miles, following cow paths, wagon roads, fording bridgeless rivers and creeks. Finally the family came upon the area of gentle rolling hills that reminded them of their native Georgia homeland Pilot Grove, Texas, located twenty miles south of the Red River that forms a natural border between Texas and Oklahoma, which was a strange unknown land full of savage and unpredictable "Red Men."

Pilot Grove, Texas, was the oldest settlement in the area, with a way station for the stage coach line. In Thomas Noel Binion's judgment, the land was suitable for raising cotton. He purchased a parcel of land from the Adams family on Pilot Grove Creek facing the stage line road referred to locally as "the Skillet." A short section of this road was later renamed Binion Road where it intersects with Brewer Road (another pioneer family name of the area). A Texas Historical Site sign marks the location of the original Binion purchase. Descendants of both the Binion and the Lee family occupy the restored home. Steve and Leslie Coker are current residents in the home and they proudly display a sign denoting the Sixth Generation Ranch.

Regardless of the treaty signed at the courthouse in Appomattox by Robert E. Lee, the plantation lifestyle of Pilot Grove remained the same. For them the war was not over.

Pilot Grove was often referred to as "Lickskillet" because of the poverty and hunger experienced by the people during the war years of 1861–1865. Four counties created a Four Corners area consisting of Grayson County, Fannin to the east, Hunt located southeast, and Collin County directly south. This was responsible for Pilot Grove being referred to as "the Corners" by the locals, as it was located where the corners of the four counties came together.

A FIGHT IN THE MULE BARN

Now step back in time as the old man in the rocking chair continues to doze, remembering: Town dogs bark as they chase the spinning yellow hubs of a green coal wagon with high sideboards and two number 2 coal scoops attached one at each side. A teenage Benny Binion cracks a whip over the mules and shouts, "Eeeeee Haaaw!"

The empty wide-wheeled wagon, traveling too fast, careens, throwing a cloud of dust and dirt into the air as it turns into the Whitewright coal yard. Benny stands as he maneuvers, pulling back on the reins, hollering, "Back!—Back!" The mules back the wagon between two mountains of coal. When they stop, Benny and Jack, his younger brother by two years, bounce from the wagon seat and grab the coal scoops, each attacking the mountain of coal on his side of the wagon. Benny flings a scoop of coal into the wagon and begins a cadence count. Standing on the porch of the yardmaster's office with other men, Benny's uncle Bill, the yardmaster, a jovial, middle-aged man, watches the boys. He speaks to an elderly, balding, bespeckled man standing next to him, "Those boys are my nephews, Alma and Lonnie Binion's boys. You just watch 'em. They'll go like hell till they get that wagon loaded. Then they'll head for the ice house."

The cadence count continues, and finally Benny shouts, "Four hundred and twenty-two—that's another load of coal for Uncle Eddy's boilers at the syrup mill, little brother." The boys put the scoops back in the slots on the side of the wagon, giving the bailing wire a twist to hold them secure. Grimy with coal dust, Benny goes to the coal yard office and signs a voucher for the load of coal. He climbs back onto the driver's seat and popping the reins on the mules' backs and calls to them as the wagon lumbers from the coal yard toward the icehouse. Benny, clucking his tongue, "Come on, Claude—git up now, Maud."As the wagon approaches the icehouse, Jack points to a swaggering Billy Hobbs, the town bully, a large boy wearing a straw hat with a turkey feather stuck at a cocky angle. Hobbs is followed by two other boys. They are older and larger than the Binion boys."Well, would you look at that idiot taking on as if he's the cock of the walk." Benny pulls the mules to a halt, and Jack jumps down and ties the mules to a hitching rail. The boys start for the icehouse and refreshments. Hobbs steps out, blocking their path. "Did you Pilot Grove sharecroppers get permission to come to town and watch the train come in?" "Don't want none of your trouble, Hobbs. Get out of my way."

Laughing and growling at the same time, Hobbs gives the smaller boy Jack a shove out into the street. Losing his balance, Jack catches the side of the coal wagon to keep from falling. His hand closes around a lump of coal. He hurls it at Hobbs. Dodging the missile, Hobbs loses his hat. Red-faced and angry, Hobbs picks up a dried horse turd and shouts, "You're in for it now—I'm gonna make you eat shit, ya little fart."

A crowd gathers. Jack, unabashed, doesn't hesitate. Making a running lunge, he tackles Hobbs, knocking him backward. The momentum and the surprise doesn't last long and Hobbs is soon sitting astride Jack, poking a horse turd toward Jack's mouth. Benny picks up Hobbs's hat with its dangling turkey feather and shoves it over Hobbs's face. A ripple of laughter comes from the crowd as Benny slaps Hobbs hard on the side of his head that sends him rolling off of Jack while some of the crowd laughs and hoots at this antic. Benny helps Jack up quickly as Hobbs's two cronies help Hobbs up. He quickly spins to face Benny.

Hobbs and Benny begin to circle each other, fists up. Hobbs motions to Benny. Shouting for Benny to come on, "I'll make you candy-ass farm boys wish you'd never come to town." Benny shifts his weight to his right foot and waits. Hobbs hollers, "Come on, sharecropper, let's see what ya got!"

Angry Hobbs snarls, "Come on... whatcha waiting for? You backwoods farm boys shoulda never come to town!" Hobbs lunges at Binion and is met with a straight right jab from Benny. The crowd gasps at this, some applauding Benny. Hobbs screams, holding his nose, "Aaghh!"

He starts to charge Benny again, but a local bartender intervenes, stepping in between the two combatants. "Whoa! Hold on, hold on!" He paused to make sure riled combatants are listening. "You can't just have a fight in the middle of our street in our town! We've got ways to settle disputes! We're not barbarians; we're civilized people, right?" The crowd responds with various nods and gestures of agreement.

The bartender, putting his arms down, says, "I mean, seriously, boys—before we go punchin' and kickin' and fightin' each other... we gotta first make some rules and get some bets down!" The crowd cheers at this fine gesture of "civilization."

Benny looks at his brother Jack, smiles, and winks. Half the male population of Whitewright follows the boys and the bartender into the mule barn. Once inside, two buckets of water and two stools are positioned, one in each corner of a large stall.

The bartender steps in between the boys and asks, "What are the rules?"Hobbs responds, "No holds barred."

Benny grins and nods affirmatively.

Bartender: "Any quarter?"

Hobbs: "None asked, none given."

Men gather shoulder to shoulder in the mule barn. Money changes hands as they argue, over the odds. Hobbs is the favorite. The only one who bets on Benny is his uncle Bill. Hobbs stands glaring. Benny simply grins, but his blue eyes are cold. The barkeeper removes the stools and water buckets from the stall and over the noise from the crowd. The bartender hollers, "Time!"The opponents begin circling each other. Hobbs tries to get a hold on Benny, but Benny keeps hitting Hobbs with either a straight right jab or a left hook. The stinging blows frustrate more than hurt Hobbs. Each time Hobbs takes a blow from Benny, Hobbs's friends groan and gasp. A spectator, a thin old man with a patch over one eye, jostles another spectator to get a better look and says excitedly, "Just last week, Hobbs bit off part of Sam Shipley's ear and spit it out to win a close fight."Benny, a teenage boy with all the moves and coolness of a professional boxer, has the back and arms of a man. He stays in the middle of the stall. When Hobbs tries to pin him with a rush, Benny keeps away from the corners. He only allows himself to be pushed toward the sides of the stall where he rolls away from Hobbs's rush, nailing him with a right hand. Eventually, Hobbs manages to get a headlock on Benny and quickly uses the advantage to get a stranglehold.

Benny runs his hand deep into his pocket. Passing his hands behind him, Benny opens the blade of his knife and plunges it into the inner thigh of Hobbs, pulling the blade down toward Hobbs's knee. Hobbs bellows in pain and momentarily loosens his grip, and Benny's knife bites into Hobbs again, close to the same place. Benny is surprised by how hot the blood rushing from Hobbs's wound is.

Pushing Hobbs aside, Benny opens the stall gate. The

wrought-up crowd parts as Benny walks out. Someone says, "It's about time someone brought that bully down to size." Benny stops at a watering trough long enough to rinse the blood from his knife and splash water on his face. The sound of a troop train as it whistles its approach to Whitewright can be heard in the distance. A young boy runs from the barn and down the main street to the town marshal's office. The town marshal, a tall well-built man, sits at his desk reading wanted posters. The young boy bursts through the door eyes wide and out of breath.

"There's a fight in the mule barn and Benny Binion pulled his knife and killed Billy Hobbs." The marshal gets up from his desk and straps two six-shooters to his side and steps out to the porch.

"Whoa now, boy—are you sure Hobbs is dead?"

"Gee, I don't know, Sheriff, but there sure is a lot of blood."

The marshal takes his hat from the wall. "You go get Doc Freeman, and I'll go see about Billy Hobbs."

At the railroad water tower, the troop train grinds to a halt taking on water. Soon the train's water tank is topped off and the engineer gives the whistle two good pulls as the train slowly moves forward.

Benny swings onto the last car. Meanwhile back in the mule barn, Uncle Bill collects on his bets as a loser protests. "I never thought that young feller would pull his knife, that doesn't seem fair." Taking his money, Uncle Bill says, "It was Hobbs himself that said no holds barred. That means clubs, knives, kicking, biting, and eye-gouging, anything but a gun." As Benny's brother Jack leaves the barn, he mounts the coal wagon seat. A loser asks, "Who were those boys anyway?" Uncle Bill watches Jack drive out of sight and says, "They're Lonnie Binion's boys. Ben Lester was the fighter and Jack is his younger brother."

DICE ON THE TROOP TRAIN

No one on the troop train notices as Benny swings aboard. The conductor, a balding stocky middle-aged man, is busy at the other end of the car. The train is packed with young soldiers. Drawing closer, Benny recognizes the game that the soldiers are playing. The conductor pushes his way through the crowded aisle, paying no attention to Benny. An army footlocker has been placed across the aisle. The dice are thrown against the side of the footlocker and bounce to a stop on the floor of the coach as the young gamblers shout, venting their emotions. Benny watches as a new shooter takes the dice. The conductor takes a quarter from the game and drops it in a coffee can. Benny notices the more experienced shooters are placing their bets after the first roll. When the dice come to Benny, he passes his turn to shoot and fades the next shooter. By the time the train reaches McKinney, Benny's pockets are stuffed with money. When he leaves the game, a soldier follows him. "You did pretty good, pardner. We only make twenty-one dollars a month and you must have over a year's wages stuffed in your pocket."

Benny nods and smiles. "I guess I just got lucky—seems I could do nothing wrong." When Benny steps from the moving train, it is early afternoon in McKinney, Texas. The main street is crowded with mules, wagons, horses, and buggies. A banner strung across the street reads MCKINNEY FIRST MONDAY TRADE DAY. The local farmers are in town to barter crops, tools, animals, or whatever they might have. Benny sees just what he wants, a matched pair of black mares and a buggy. A For Sale or Trade sign hangs from the rear of the buggy. Benny walks over to the mares and examines their teeth, then runs his hands over their necks and shoulders. He picks up the front hoof of each animal. The owner watches as Benny continues his appraisal of the buggy as well.

"What are you asking for the rig?"

"I got $300 in 'em—I'll take $250."

Benny turns and starts to walk away.

"Make me an offer, young feller."

Benny returns, approaches the owner, and sticks out his hand. "Sir, my name is Ben Lester Binion. I can pay you two hundred dollars cash for the mares and buggy."

"I'll take two hundred and twenty-five dollars."

"Two hundred's all I got." The owner stares intently at Benny, shifts a wad of tobacco from one side of his mouth to the other, and spits. "You drive a hard bargain, son!"

The two men shake hands. Benny turns his back and takes a roll of money from his pocket and counts out two hundred dollars and shoves the rest deep down in his pocket. Turning back around, Benny hands the money to the owner, who takes the sign off the back of the buggy as Benny climbs into the seat and takes the reins. "Treat 'em kindly, son."

Later that afternoon, the buggy follows a country lane and approaches a one-story white-framed home with a circular gravel driveway and a wide front porch. Benny turns in past a mailbox with the name Dave Taylor. He drives his new team and buggy into the yard, circling the drive in front of his six young cousins on the porch. In awe, and wide-eyed, the boys whistle softly. The mares' coats are brushed smooth as velvet, the harness oiled and polished.

"Whoa! Where's Uncle Dave?"

"Mom and Dad are in McKinney for Trade Day."Benny circles the team again, stopping long enough for the cousins to pat the mares. The boys gather around the buggy as Benny lowers his voice. "Someday, I'm gonna come back with a Cadillac automobile."

Later approaching the Binion home, the hounds run out barking not recognizing the black mares and buggy. Benny drives the buggy into the barn. Lonnie, Benny's dad, walks into the barn while Benny is unhitching the mares. Lonnie runs his hand over the shoulder of the closest mare.

"That's a mighty fine-looking rig. Who does it belong to, son?"

"They're mine, Dad. I bought them with money I won gambling."

"What kind of gambling, son?"

"I got into a dice game on the troop train that came through Whitewright."

"Benny, no good is gonna come of your gambling."

Lonnie takes the harness from the mares and hangs it on the barn wall. "Jack brought the coal wagon back from Whitewright. He said you did a number on the Hobbs boy." Benny keeps working with the mares, brushing them as his father talks. "He told us about the fight. The Hobbs boy had forty-seven stitches taken in his leg and his face looks like hamburger meat. Jack told me Hobbs says he's gonna kill you."

Benny continued to brush the mares and, without looking up, said, "I gave Hobbs a message when I cut him on the leg. I could have opened him up just as easy to see what he had for breakfast. If he's dumb enough to come after me, we'll just have to see who's the meanest." Shaking his head, Lonnie suppresses a smile. "Supper's ready. Wash up and come up to the house. Don't keep your ma waiting."Later that next morning, Benny, Jack, and Lonnie sit at the kitchen table drinking coffee. They had just finished breakfast. Benny's younger sister, Dorothy, and his mother, Alma, are clearing the table and doing the dishes.

"Dad, Jack's old enough now to make the coal run to Whitewright. One of the Stinnet boys can ride with him to help load the coal." Benny continues and Lonnie leans back in his chair and studies his son. "The gambling on that troop train, compared to Pilot Grove, is easy pickings. I've decided to become a gambler, maybe I'll join the army. Someday, I'm gonna come back to see you driving a Cadillac."

"Son, I hate to see you do that. Gambling is the meanest way in the world to make a living. If you're lucky enough to come out a winner—and that may not happen, you'll have to carry a gun—sooner or later some hijacker, or gambler, or sore loser will try to take your money, maybe your life." Lonnie stares out the kitchen window for a moment, then with a worried look, returns his attention to Benny. "I've seen a lot of men leave, saying they were gonna gamble for a living—and they all came back broke. Sooner or later you'll be in a shooting scrape—you'll either kill someone or be killed." Benny's cold blue-eyed stare meets his father's, and Lonnie knows it's no use to try to dissuade his young son.

"I just need a ride to the train station, Dad. There'll be another troop train coming through today."

Later that morning, Lonnie, shoulders hunched, silently drives the new buggy, Benny beside him. The wind blows brightly colored leaves skittering across the road under the buggy and the hooves of the frisky black mares as they approach the Whitewright train station. As they say good-bye, the old man chokes back a tear. When Lonnie leaves the station in the buggy and starts for home, he turns to see Benny standing on the loading dock while the troop train takes on water.

Benny doesn't bother to buy a ticket. When the train is in motion, he swings up onto the rear platform of the last car. He enters through the back door of the car and hears the familiar sound of the clicking of dice and the voice of a shooter, "Hot damn, dice—give me a seven." The conductor, a lanky and jovial man, hovers over the players like an umpire at a baseball game. Waiting for a lull in the noise, Benny puts his hand on the conductor's shoulder.

"Sir, my name is Ben Lester Binion. I got on the train without a ticket."

The conductor looks at Benny and grins.

"My name is Jeff. I tell ya what, kid—give me a dollar and we'll call it even. You go up to the commissary car and tell the porter that Jeff wants a sandwich and a cup of coffee."

"Yes, sir, right away."

When Benny returns with the sandwich and coffee for the conductor, Jeff asks.

"You want a job, son?"

"You bet, what's the job?"

"Have you ever shot dice?"

"Sir, I've been shooting dice since Tige was a pup."

"OK, stay here and take a quarter out of the pot each time a new shooter takes the dice and drop it in the coffee can. What did you say your name was, kid?"

"Ben Lester Binion, sir."

"OK, I'll call you Benny. Watch my game now while I eat my sandwich."

Benny watches the game and soon learns the names of the players and gives verbal encouragement to the shooters and sympathy to the losers as the troop train rumbles toward Ft. Worth. In addition to collecting a quarter each time a new shooter took the dice, Benny makes some bets for himself.

He fades the shooters, winning more often than losing,

and stuffs the money in his pocket. His charisma and his Texas gambling lingo add luster to the game. As the dice pass, Benny sings out, "New shooter coming out for a new point. Bobby Brooks, the bugler boy, coming out for a new point." The company bugler rolls a five. "Bobby's point is five, Bobby is looking for a five, five will be a winner!"

Benny has a saying for every point and roll of the dice. When the dice showed an eight, Benny sang out, "What did Bobby roll? It's an eighter from Decatur, county seat of Wise, eight easy eight, a three and a five."

A crowd gathers around Benny's game just to hear his vocal analysis as a shooter makes his point. Nudging each other, they crowd in closer to watch the action. As Bobby rolls another five, Benny chants, "Five a Winner! Winner! Winner!" When a shooter sevens out, Benny sings out, "Bad old seven— craps—It's all away."

Time flies and the lights are turned on as the train rumbles through the evening and into the night. Jeff enters the car and stands at the door. "There'll be a two-hour stop in Ft. Worth."

A sergeant steps into the car and blows his drill whistle to get attention. "There will be a muster and roll call outside the train. The Red Cross has set up coffee and sandwiches for you men."

Through the train car window, Benny could see the men assemble for roll call.

Benny finds Jeff and a porter seated at a desk in the conductor's office. Benny empties the quarters from the coffee can. Jeff quickly counts the quarters into stacks of ten, then shoves four stacks toward Benny. "You're doing great, kid— keep the ten bucks. If you want to keep working the game, we can sure use you."

Benny grinned. "You bet. Where is this train headed anyway?"

"We'll be in El Paso some time day after tomorrow. It's about a thirty-six-hour trip."

The next day, while sandwiches were being passed out for the noon meal, Benny asks the sergeant if he can join the army and stay with the company. The sergeant has observed that Benny is an accomplished gambler and suspects there would be trouble later on. He explained to Benny that there would be paperwork to joining the army, and without a birth certificate and the proper credentials, he couldn't get him on the company's roster.

That night after revelry, Jeff once again counts out Benny's quarters and slides the pile toward Benny. As Benny rises to leave, Jeff stands and puts his hand on Benny's shoulder. "Early tomorrow, we are stopping in El Paso, the end of the line. Benny, you're going to have to watch your back. El Paso is full of meanness. Town bullies are running El Paso to suit themselves. The town attracts all kinds of riffraff, rustlers, and mean desperadoes. And just across the Rio Grande is Juarez, Mexico, ideally situated for anyone on the dodge. But on the other side of the scale are some of the toughest and meanest lawmen in the territory. Frank Bass, an ex–Texas Ranger, is town marshal, and Bobby MC Cord is chief of police. MC Cord's motto is "If anybody in this town needs killing, I'll do it."

EL PASO, TEXAS

Early the next morning, Benny steps from the troop train. A sergeant blows his drill whistle, and the soldiers fall into ranks outside the train. His pockets stuffed with money, Benny walks from the railroad station into the streets of El Paso. The city is raucous with noise the clopping of horse's hooves and clattering of wagon wheels, the clanging of streetcars, barking dogs, braying of a donkey and an occasional automobile horn.

Music blares from every saloon door, along with rink-a-tink piano and Mexican hurdy-gurdy tunes all off-key. Benny stops to watch an old Mexican woman who squats outside her door, patting tortillas. Beans boil in a pot on a small charcoal fire. He passes old women in black rebozos, their faces dry and cracked, hunkered on the sidewalks, their bony hands outstretched for coins. He places a quarter in each outstretched hand. He wanders on to a fruit stand. The proprietor polishes his fruit.

"What's the best hotel in town with a bath?"

The proprietor looks at Benny, wipes his hands on his apron. "The very finest hotel is the Encerno Hotel across the river in Juarez. Just cross the bridge—stay on the main road and you'll see it."

In the lobby of the hotel is a beautiful marble floor, potted palm trees, and a winding white staircase leading to the mezzanine. Benny negotiates the price of a room with a bath. The manager hands Benny a key and rings a bell on the countertop for a bellhop. He follows the bellhop up the stairway to a room on the second floor. The bellhop opens the door to a spacious room with an ornate bed, a large bath, and a balcony overlooking a flowering patio. Satisfied, he tips the bellhop.

After a nap and a hot bath, Benny dresses and goes outside to a line of carriages for hire; he approaches the first carriage.

The driver is a smiling small Mexican man. Benny steps up into the carriage. "Take me to the best clothing store in Juarez, amigo."

"Si, señor, con gusto."

The driver cracks his whip and the pony jerks the carriage forward; then he stops a few blocks away in front of a clothing store with large French doors.

Inside, a clerk, a thin man with shifty eyes, showed Benny to a fitting room. He assists Benny in the selection of a handsome jacket and a pair of boots. He helps Benny into the jacket and then surprises Benny when he produced a .38 Colt automatic wrapped in oilcloth. "This is a very special jacket. If you are going to stay in Juarez, señor, I recommend you wear a jacket like this one."

Benny examined the pistol and then slides it into the pocket. Facing a mirror, he grins as he draws the pistol smoothly and quickly.

Back at his hotel, Benny pitches his bundles on a chair and collapses onto the bed, fully dressed, and falls into a deep sleep. Upon awakening, later that evening, Benny practices his quick draw from the new jacket pocket. Satisfied, he buttons his jacket and leaves. Benny steps into the streets of Juarez and whistles for a passing carriage.

"Where would you like to go, señor?"

"Show me the Juarez nightlife."

"Excellent choice, señor."

With a crack of the whip, the carriage passes through the babbling, bustling streets of Juarez. They pass bars and many beautiful girls in gaily-colored dresses. A large green sign in the shape of a cactus hangs at a cantina entrance. Manuel, a handsome enthusiastic young boy, approaches from the open door of the cantina and takes hold of the horse's bridle. Manuel gestures toward the cantina. "Come inside, señor, for a free drink and an evening of high adventure!"

He paid the carriage driver and followed Manuel into the Cantina Verde. They passed through a large carved dark oak door with beautiful colored glass. Manuel leads the way into a ballroom with a large silver ornament that sends out rays of light hanging from the thick oak ceiling beams.

Benny sees beautiful young girls sitting at a table. The girls giggle and whisper to each other, making eyes at Benny as he passes. One rises from her chair and stalks Benny like she is going to grab him, then turns and slips back to her table. Manuel holds a chair for Benny and then signals a waiter in a short white jacket who brings Benny a margarita. A bartender watches with interest and sends a young boy with a message, scurrying into the street. A waiter leans over the table serving a margarita. "Compliments of the house, señor."

Benny responds, "Mochas gracias, hombre."

At a table not far away, Mickey, a beautiful young girl with sparkling eyes and dimples, speaks to Maria, a dark-haired beauty, nodding toward Benny. "I have to have that one, but I must be quick and bold, or one of the other girls will beat me to him."

Benny is watching a large parrot perched on a golden loop

behind the bar. Mickey suddenly comes up on Benny's blind side and straddles his lap. She smiles as she brazenly pushes her breast into Benny's chest. Mickey whispers into Benny's ear, "Hi, my name is Mickey. Would you like to buy me a drink?"

When their eyes meet, Benny falls in love at first sight. Mickey snuggles closer, putting her arms around Benny, caressing the back of his neck with her fingers. Benny grins as he runs his hand under her dress along a shapely bare thigh.

"Mickey, my friends call me Benny, and I want us to be friends!"

Benny motions to a waiter.

"Bring my lady friend Mickey a drink."

The waiter asks, "What would you like, Señorita Mickey?"

"Un margarita, por favor."

A mariachi band is playing. There are only a few customers in the cantina.

Mickey asks, "Benny, do you like to dance?"

"I never learned how. Would you teach me?"

"Oh yes, but let's wait for the right kind of music."

Mickey motions to Maria, who comes to their table and takes a chair. Mickey giggles and looks at Benny. "Benny doesn't know how to dance. We're going to teach him." Mickey, looking at Benny shyly from beneath lush black lashes, whispers in Maris's ear, "I think Benny's a virgin!"

Maria goes to the musicians and makes a request and motions toward Benny's table. The musicians smile and nod. Mickey rises and Benny follows her to the dance floor. A violin and an accordion are paced by a slow sultry drumbeat. Mickey wraps herself around Benny. As the evening wears on, the cantina fills with more customers. The girls take turns dancing close with Benny.

While Benny is dancing with Maria, Rafael, owner of the cantina, arrives and sits down at the table with Mickey.

Rafael is an older man with refined Spanish appearance and manners.

"What have you learned about your young gringo friend, Mickey? Is he a deserter from the army?"

"No, Patron—he is not a soldier—just another young gringo having a good time away from his ranch."

"Ask him if he is interested in making some quick money and see what he has to say."

"When it is right, I will ask him."

Benny and Maria return to the table. Rafael stands as Benny holds a chair for Maria. "Benny, this is Rafael, my patron and the owner of Cantina Verde."

Smiling, showing perfect white teeth, Rafael bows from the waist, straightens, and extends his hand. "Mickey told me all about you, Benny. You are from Texas and you know all about horses and now I see my girls are teaching you all about how to dance."

"These girls are a lot more fun than the horses. Will you join our party? I want us to be friends."

"Why certainly, it would be my pleasure."

Rafael takes the chair next to Maria and across from Benny.

"Is this your first trip to Mexico?"

"Yes, it is—I like it so much, I'm going to buy it and put a fence around it." They laugh at Benny's jest. A flirtatious young girl comes to the table, takes Benny by the hand, and leads him to the dance floor. She clings sensuously to him while they dance. Watching the dance, Rafael says, "When Benny comes back to the table, Mickey—you and Maria go to the powder room so that Benny and I can talk in private."

When Benny returns, the girls all leave for the powder room.

Rafael asks, "Are you having a good time, Benny?"

"Yes, yes, I am. So you own this place, eh?"

"Yes, I am what they call the patron."

Jesting Benny asks, "Would you consider selling me the business?"

Leaning back in his chair, Rafael hits the table with an open palm, making a loud whack. "Benny, you are my kind of man—muy macho. No, the business is not for sale, but I will make you a partner in an operation that I'm putting together."

Benny laughs and hollers, "Ieeeeee, well you would have of had to carry my note anyway, Ieeeeee."

"Can we talk serious, Benny, or have you had too much to drink?" Benny pulls his hand over his smiling face, and when the hand is removed, the smile has been replaced with a sober look. "If you want to talk about making money, I'm deadly serious."

BUSINESS AND PLEASURE
IN JUAREZ

RAFAEL LOWERS HIS voice and moves to the chair next to Benny leaning close. "Good! There is a tremendous opportunity here in Juarez, if we can make the right connection with the Texas railroad." He offers a cigar and both men light up. The girls and the musicians watch from across the room. "Crossing the Mexican border is no problem. Transportation to the U.S. interior is the problem." A girl starts toward Benny's table from the restroom. Mickey intercepts her and turns her away.

Rafael continues, "With the right connections with the Texas railroads, we could move the mescal and tequila out of Mexico and smuggle guns in, taking a commission both ways. Do you think you could find such a man with the railroad?"

"If I set this up, what is my part?"

"Your part would be five percent for you and five percent for a railroad connection."

Taking his cigar from his mouth, Benny waits a moment before answering. "I don't think that is going to be enough of an incentive for the railroad connection—after all, he's laying his job on the line, with possible jail time."

"Get an indication of interest and the commission can be negotiated."

"How much business do you think could be done in a year?"

"We could do something in excess of a million dollars if everything goes well."

"I have a man in mind with the railroad, but it will take money all along the way to provide the right incentive."

"Then you will do this thing?"

Benny extends his hand to Rafael and pulls him close with the handshake. "We are partners, Rafael. Do you know what that means to a Texan?"

"No, Benny—tell me."

Squeezing Rafael's hand hard, Benny says, "It means if you fuck me over—I'll stick my pistol up your ass and pull the trigger! Ieeeeee."

Rafael, laughing, says, "I see that you are, indeed, a cunning businessman, Benny."

The two men clink glasses. As if the toast were a signal, Mickey returns to the table. Benny puts out his cigar as Rafael leaves the table. Mickey takes Benny by the hand and leads him to a door at the rear of the cantina. A beautiful huge moon hangs low in the sky and a patio fountain splashes into a holding pool. Doors to rooms line the perimeter of the patio. Mickey leads Benny to one of the doors.

"Do you have a knife, Benny?"

Benny opens his pocketknife and gives it to Mickey. She slides the blade along the door jamb till she finds the latch. Pushing the blade inward, the latch clicks and Mickey cracks the door just enough to let them see into the room. Mickey kneels down so Benny can see over her shoulder. A candle is burning on a table in front of a mirror and gives off a soft light that reveals a handsome young man lying on his back, his head and shoulders propped up with pillows. A beautiful young girl is sitting astraddle him, slowly and provocatively working her hips as he groans, "Right there."

The young man growls with pleasure as he plucks at her bare nipples. Looking up at Benny, Mickey says, "My, what a nice love muscle you have," giving him a squeeze. Benny pulls Mickey up by her hair, then they share a deep kiss. Pulling away taking Benny's hand, Mickey says, "Follow me."

Mickey unlocks the door to room number 5, enters, and lights a candle in front of her mirror. Then she kneels at a small shrine of Mother Mary, says a short prayer, and then crosses herself. She stands and turns toward Benny and slowly, seductively, drops her dress from her shoulders. Mickey smiles at Benny as he watches intently.

She gently pushes him back on the bed, removes his boots, and pulls his trousers off one leg at a time and hangs them over the back of a chair.

A group of girls from the cantina quietly unlock Mickey's door, peeping in, giggling and whispering. They are watching as Benny pulls Mickey onto the bed and mounts her as Mickey guides with her hand. "Ay, chihuahua—be careful with that thing, big boy—easy now—right there. Now, Benny—push right there—Yes, yes—yesss!"

Benny is quick as a gunshot, but he is ready to go again and again. Finally they lie together exhausted. Mickey snuggles and says, "You're everything I hoped you would be, the man I've always dreamed of."

"Mickey, I don't want you working here anymore. I'm gonna make a lot of money and take you away from all this." She buries her head in Benny's chest.

Mickey and Benny return to the dance hall. A bugle blares and the band strikes up "The March of the Toreadors." The dance hall girls all clap and chant, "Benny! Benny! Benny!" He takes it good-naturedly and joins in the fun, strutting and striking the pose of a victorious matador, bowing in all directions and blowing kisses to the squealing girls.

Early the next morning, Benny drives a wagon, loaded with wooden crates, marked Singer Sewing Machines to the side of a waiting boxcar. Jeff and the freight train conductor, a large older man with shaggy gray salt-and-pepper hair and beard, called the *Shack* nod to Benny. Four Mexican workers scramble out of the empty boxcar and begin loading the wooden crates.

A DISPUTED POKER HAND

As THE SUN sets that evening, Benny sits at a poker table with four other men. A well-dressed elderly gentleman talks with a group of men at the bar. "That young gambler is getting a reputation as a hell of a poker player and has earned the distinction of being a reckless card player. It seems he can't lose. Tonight, though, his luck is not holding and he is losing big time." Benny's disposition becomes surly. He is in no mood for the joshing and goading going on at the table.

Sonny Dixon, a small blond man, always smiling, lays down four tens to take the biggest pot of the night, a pot Benny felt sure he was going to take with a full house, three jacks over a pair of fives—it was just too much for Benny, he stands and shouts, "Damn you, Sonny!" He grabs Sonny's cards and sends them flying across the room and, with a well-coordinated move of his left hand, at the same time drawing his .38 Colt automatic with his right hand. Everyone at the table talks at once.

"Hey now, no need for that, Benny!"

Benny glares at Billy Bates who dealt the hand and hollers, "Bates, I've had enough of your dealing seconds!"

"It ain't my dealing that's costing you, Benny—it's your playing."

"Save your bullshit for your Sunday school class, Bates."

Benny holds the pistol in one hand and scoops up the money with his other hand. "The whole lot of ya been playing me for a sucker all night, but this game is over now and the pot's mine. Anybody got any objections—all ya gotta do is make a move."

No one moves as Benny stuffs the money in his pockets and leaves. As soon as he is out of sight, Billy Bates says, "I'm gonna get the law."

Frank Bass, the town marshal, a tall strong man in his late sixties, graying at the temples, listens to the disgruntled gambler. Then he and Billy Bates leave the saloon.

They walk toward Ciudad, Juarez, and the Encerno Hotel when they spot Benny at the bar in the Red Door Saloon. Frank Bass steps up to Benny at the bar. "Mr. Binion, you're under arrest for robbing a card game."

Benny snaps, "I just took what belongs to me, Bass."

"Well, come along. You can tell your story to Judge Sanders and let him sort it out."

Benny, mad and red in the face, shouts, "I'm just telling you what happened, Bass!"

The people at the bar in the line of fire quickly move out of the way. Bobby McCord, chief of police, a wiry, mean-looking man, enters the saloon. "I heard the story from Bates. If you can prove he was dealing seconds, I'll do something about it, but if you can't, then you're in the wrong taking the money and you know it."

"I know I've been cheated, but I can't prove it."

Frank Bass with his hand on his holstered pistol says, "Then I'll have to arrest you for robbery, Mr. Binion, and I'll have to have your pistol."

Benny steps back glaring at Bass and squares off for a fight. "You're not gonna take my pistol, you murdering old bastard. I've heard about the way you treat prisoners." Benny motions to the chief of police. "I'll surrender to Chief McCord."

Frank Bass stares at Benny, his eyes blazing.

Later Benny stands before Judge Sanders, a stern middle-aged portly man. The judge bangs his gavel. " You must return the disputed money to the balif and that will be a twenty-five dollars for disturbing the peace, young man." Benny pulls a large roll of bills from his pocket and leaves for the Cantina Verde and Mickey.

THE .38 COLT AUTOMATIC
ROARS THREE TIMES

WITH THE EXCEPTION of an occasional dog barking, the town is quiet as he approaches the cantina. Benny pauses in the entrance of the cantina and looks around. A clock on the wall shows a little past 4:00 a.m. Rafael is playing cards with some of the locals. He spots a friend at the bar, Joe Stone, a stocky young man in need of a shave. Benny mounts a barstool next to Joe and asks, "How long you been here, Joe?"

"I been playing cards with Rafael all night."

"How did you make out?"

Joe finishes his tequila, reaches in his shirt pocket, and takes out a Bull Durham sack and some cigarette papers. "That's all I got left."

Benny nods to the bartender and holds up two fingers. Turning back to Joe, Benny asks, "Have you seen Mickey?"

"Haven't seen her all night."

"What kind of game is Rafael playing?"

"Pot limit, five-card stud."

The bartender serves tequilas; Benny puts some money on the bar and takes his drink to the card table. Rafael looks up and grins. "We got room for one more, Benny."

"I'm looking for Mickey. Have you seen her?"

"No, I have been too busy reading my cards to know what's going on. Find Manuel—he'll help you."

Benny looks around the cantina, but Manuel is nowhere in sight. Benny goes out the rear door of the cantina. He sits by a splashing fountain, sipping his tequila. A pale light is beginning to glow in the east. Another rooster crows, then another, as Benny tilts his glass and finishes his tequila. Manuel enters the patio and asks, "Are you are looking for Mickey, Señor Benny?"

"Yeah, do you know where she is?"

"She is no longer in Juarez, Señor Benny."

Benny lurches from his chair and grabs Manuel by the shirt collar and growls, "What the hell do you mean she's no longer in Juarez?"

Realizing he is hurting the smaller man, Benny releases his grip. "You will have to ask Rafael. Perhaps he can help you."

A wave of anger surges through Benny, and he growls, "I know a Mexican runaround when I get one. First Rafael says find Manuel—now you tell me find Rafael."

Benny returns to the cantina. Everyone is gone; in a blind rage, he goes behind the bar and into the quarters at the rear. He finds it empty too. He returns to the patio and kicks open the door of Mickey's room. He finds Mickey's friend Maria in bed with a man. She grabs a sheet to cover her naked body, her eyes big as saucers. Benny doesn't notice a federal cavalry officer's red britches with a gold stripe folded neatly on a bedside chair. Benny shouts, "Maria, what has happened to Mickey, what the hell is going on? Where is Mickey?"

Maria is petrified. The cavalry officer, a handsome young man with a neatly trimmed moustache, rolls to the side of the bed and sits up. "With your permission, señor, may I put my pants on?"

Benny snaps, "Put your damn pants on and keep quiet."

Maria hides her face behind the sheet, trying to hide from the unpleasant scene. "Maria, what has happened to Mickey—where is she?"

As the cavalry officer picks up his pants, his hand closes on a pistol and holster under his trousers. He takes a firm grip on the holster and jerks the pistol toward Benny. The officer's thumb is not yet on the hammer of the pistol, a single-action Colt revolver. Looking down the muzzle of the officer's pistol, a cold rage sweeps over Benny. His hand flashes to his leather pocket and the .38 Colt automatic appears as if by magic and roars three times.

Maria screams as one bullet hits the cavalry officer in the throat and the other lodges in his shoulder. He falls to the floor as the last bullet splatters into the adobe wall. Dogs bark and the sound of running feet comes from outside. "Goddamn the luck!"

Benny reaches for the door. When he opens it, two huge German shepherd dogs lunge at him. One of the dogs grabs his gun hand. As Benny tries to switch the .38 automatic to his other hand, the second dog lunges for his throat, knocking him to the floor. Rafael vaults into the room and hits Benny a vicious blow with a short heavy club, pain jolts through Benny, then he is pulled into an oblivious curtain of blackness.

A faded white sign over the door of the building reads POLICIA. Inside Benny lies on a jail cot, with one arm across his eyes. A short fat guard notices blood on Benny's pillow and enters the cell to examine him, then yells, "Medico!—Medico!" Flies buzz around Benny as the guard props him up to a sitting position. A doctor, a thin tired-looking man in a rumpled white jacket, finally arrives. As he cleans the dog bites and lacerated scalp, Benny tries to focus his eyes, but a wave of darkness comes over him. He feels cool water as his face is being carefully cleaned. Through blurred vision, he sees a doctor in a white jacket with a black bag. "You have a few lacerations. Luckily, your skull is thick and the blow did not kill you. There is no infection and you will soon heal. Can you focus your eyes—can you see all right?"

Benny tries to sit up. He feels nauseous, but manages to stand and holds on to the bars of a small window in the cell. Outside the sun is bright. Dust blows down the street. After adjusting for the bright light, he is able to focus his eyes. He grimaces. "Who are you—why am I here?"

"I am Doctor Phillip Mendez. What can you remember?"

Benny sits back down on the cot, holding his stomach, and closes his eyes. "I can remember being attacked by some dogs, and someone hit me from behind. Doc, my stomach feels queasy!"

"You need some food in your stomach. I'll have some soup brought in."

The doctor leaves, and Benny lies back down on the cot, thinking, "I know that I'm in a Mexican jail—not a good place to be. I wonder if Mickey knows where I am."

The short fat guard carries a tray with a white napkin draped over it and waits while a taller guard selects a key from a large ring full of keys and opens Benny's cell door. The short guard smiles and sets the tray on the floor while at the same time the tall guard takes a swill bucket from the cell.

"Gracias."

"Por nada, señor."

Benny takes the napkin from the tray and finds a bowl with a dish on top and a small loaf of hard bread. There is no spoon. He removes the plate covering the bowl of soup. A large black fly slowly buzzes up from the bowl.

"Damn slimy little bastard."

Benny uses his fingers to dip out a second dead fly. Taking

his time, he dips the bread into the soup, savoring every mouthful. Benny is again thinking, "The one thing these Mexicans do well is make soup."

BUSTING OUT OF A MEXICAN JAIL

LATER THAT NIGHT, Benny's stomach is cramping. He franticly searches for the swill bucket. He moves to the cell door and hollers, "Guard, bring back my pail." There is no response. Benny curls up on his cot, holding his stomach, and dozes off into a restless sleep. In the deep of night, he is awakened by men approaching with a lantern. The tall guard opens the door and the ex–Texas Ranger Frank Bass steps in and hunkers down in front of Benny, who rolls to a sitting position.

"I know you are sick, I can smell it, but what I need to know is, are you well enough to ride?"

"Yeah, but to say I've had a soft stool would be an understatement."

Frank Bass chuckles. "Yeah, Mexican squirts will kill a man if he's left in this hellhole." Frank takes a bottle of paregoric from his pocket. "Take a couple of swigs of this and it'll lock your bowls. Now listen tight—we don't have much time. I've paid the guard. My horse and one for you are right outside the window. I'm gonna run my lariat through the window and tie onto the bars." Benny takes a long swig from the bottle of paregoric. "The bars will come right out of the adobe when I kick my horse. You jump through the hole and follow me. We're gonna cross the river just below the railroad bridge. The water is shallow enough, the horses won't even have to swim—son, you are gonna owe me big time when we get you out of this hellhole, but I'll explain later."

As Frank stands to leave, Benny grabs his shoulder. "I just want to tell you one thing, Bass. You're not the murdering old bastard I thought you were."

Frank spits a stream of tobacco juice. "Wait till you hear what you owe me, Benny."

The jail door clanks shut and the jailer turns the key as Frank disappears into the darkness. Benny hears a low whistle and the rope appears through the bars. He quickly passes the end around the bars and pushes the rope back outside. The slack in the rope tightens. There is a sound of gravel scraping, but nothing happens. Then a long silence and "Pull, you son of a bitch!" A loud whack sounds as the window bars move. Adobe crumbles and falls into the street, but the bars refuse to budge. Another loud whack and the bars fly out into the night and clank against the gravel in the street. Benny scrambles through the hole into the moonlight street and mounts the horse held for him.

At a dead gallop, Frank Bass leads the way through the moonlit streets of Juarez. After putting enough distance between themselves and the jail, Frank looks back to make sure there is no one in pursuit and they slow the horses to a trot as Benny breathes a sigh of relief.

They ford the Rio Grande just below the railroad bridge and the horses climb the riverbank to the Texas side. Once in the city of El Paso, Frank leads the way to the freight yard. Frank silently nods to the freight train conductor nicknamed "Shack," a weather-beaten older man, waiting with a lantern. Frank and Benny ride their horses up a loading ramp into an empty cattle car. The men unsaddle the horses and tie them to a hitching rail at the rear of the car.

"You all set, Frank?"

"All set, Shack. Let's go."

The Shack swings his lantern as he walks forward to the engine's cab. The locomotive whistles twice and then chugs into the darkness of the night. Benny is soon asleep, his head resting on his saddle, a Stetson pulled over his eyes. Later that evening, Frank Bass looks out of the cattle car as the train whistles its approach to Laredo. "We'll be in Laredo soon, Benny. I'm starved—let's head for the Cadillac Bar and chow down."

"That sounds like a damn fine idea, Frank."

As the train slows almost to a halt, Frank swings down from the cattle car; he motions to the Shack who is standing beside the locomotive. The Shack in turn signals the engineer. Frank then mounts a loading ramp and stands motioning for the train to back to align the cattle car with Benny and the horses at the ramp. The freight train bumps to a halt. Frank jerks the cattle car door open and Benny leads the horses onto the ramp. The men mount and ride into Laredo. They check in at the livery stable. The livery manager recognizes Frank and nods toward Benny.

"Howdy, Frank—who's the stranger?"

"He's kin."

The livery manager waits, but Frank says nothing more. The livery stable manager spits a stream of tobacco juice and leads the horses away.

THE CADILLAC BAR

CROSSING A DUSTY street, bright with a white hot sun, Benny and Frank enter a cool darkened room of the Cadillac Bar. Inside are slow twirling ceiling fans. The tables are covered with white tablecloths. Waiters in starched white jackets stand with their backs to a long highly polished mahogany bar with a brass foot rail, ready to wait on customers. Locals stand at the bar, drinking and talking. A small smiling and energetic waiter approaches.

"A table for two, señor?"

Frank nods and points to a table in the rear by a door to the kitchen. The waiter in turn motions for another waiter who leads Frank and Benny to their selected table. The waiter asks, "What can I get you to drink?"

Frank responds "Cervesa"Si, señors, two beers."

The waiter hurries away to the bar. Frank lowers his voice, "I don't think we got any problem with the Mexican law here in Laredo, but you may have a price on your head in Juarez. The man you shot is still alive but he lost a lot of blood."

The waiter returns with the beer. "Are you ready to order?"

"Bring me a saddle blanket steak, rare."

Benny nods, and the waiter disappears into the kitchen. Lowering his voice, Frank leans close and says, "Ya got a problem—the man you shot is Don Diego Valdez, a captain with the federals in Juarez—and to make matters worse, his father is the local commandant. Your bootlegging and gunrunning days in Mexico are over. What did Don Diego do that riled you so?"

"The son of a bitch pointed a loaded pistol at me."

Frank smiles and nods. "Sounds like he gave you good cause."

"I was already pissed off 'cause no one would help me find Mickey. It was just the last damn straw—and when I saw his thumb start for the hammer, I made my play."

The waiter returns and serves sizzling steaks that lap over the sides of the plates.

Hungry, both men discontinue their conversation and turn their attention to the steaks. Frank wipes his chin with a napkin. "Benny, when you shot Don Diego, were you scared?"

Benny, using his fingers, takes a piece of gristle from his mouth. "I'd never looked down the muzzle of a pistol before—I felt a rush of cold rage. It seemed like everything was happening in slow motion."

Frank motions for their waiter and he returns. "Bring us a bottle of Four Roses and some cigars"—turning back to Benny—"That night in El Paso, before McCord arrested you for the disputed poker hand—you squared off against me—there was no doubt in my mind that you would have drawn on me had I pushed you further."

"You're right, Frank—I was wound tight."

Frank relights his cigar and, between puffs, says, "It's a feeling a man gets from experience, a sort of sixth sense. I made up my mind about you that night—I could see myself when I was your age. I know how a woman can get in a man's mind. But if you don't get Mickey out of your head, you're never gonna scratch anything but a poor man's ass."

The waiter returns with a bottle of Four Roses. Frank fills their glasses as he talks. "Benny, a man has to master three things in his life: drinking, gambling, and women. You handle your liquor all right and you are a winner at gambling, but you are going to have to learn to classify women. They come with three labels. Sporting girls like Mickey—you got to pay them, but they are always available. Then there are girls who can keep a secret—they're fun, but they are hard to find. Finally there are the serious girls—they're the ones that you'll raise a family with, a woman like your mother."

Benny hangs his head as Frank's words are sinking in. Frank places his hand on Benny's shoulder. "You know, Benny, young girls like Mickey are exploited, it is a way of life in Mexico. Poverty is so common that a father sometimes sells a daughter into bondage, placing her under the rule of a patron. They get 'em started on dope to control them and work 'em until the girl has repaid the father's debt."

Obviously distressed, Benny asks, "Do you really think that Mickey is on dope?"

"Know damn well she is—that's the way Rafael controls her. She has probably been moved to another city because she was getting sweet on you and she didn't want to turn tricks with the regulars."

Holding his face in his hands, Benny sobs gently. "And that damn Rafael was the one giving the orders. He's the son of a bitch that hit me on the head."

Frank finishes his glass of whiskey. "Now you got the picture. Benny, if I thought you'd ever sell drugs or work women, I'd leave you in that jail to rot."

"What do you think will happen to Mickey?"

"She doesn't have a Chinaman's chance in hell. I'd bet she's been shipped inland, maybe to Chihuahua City. She'll be fresh meat for the locals."

Benny hits the table with a closed fist as Frank pours him another whiskey. "Hold your head up, Benny—this will pass."

BUGGER RED

A SMALL COWBOY enters the Cadillac Bar. He stands a mere five feet, four inches tall and weighs 145 pounds at the most. His pale Irish face is badly scarred from burns and his gray hair is tousled. Small feet encased in size 4 boots are held up by stubby legs bowed from bronc riding. He is followed by Ray Chadwick, lean, dark hair, with pitted face, and Bobby McGhee, a jolly redhead cowboy with his Stetson pulled low. The smaller cowboy looks around and is surprised to see his old compatriot and walks straight to Frank's table. "Frank Bass—what in hell are you doing in Laredo? Are you and your gang here to rob the Laredo bank?"

"Bugger Red—if you aren't a sight for sore eyes—where's the rodeo?"

Benny quickly regains his composure and stands as the men introduce themselves. "You boys grab a chair and join Benny and me."

"Ain't no rodeo. The army's paying us to break some mustangs." Bugger gestures to the waiter. "Hey, amigo. Bring

42

us three beers." Bugger turns back to Frank. "Just got off the train—me and the boys wanted to wet our whistle before we go to work."

Later at the corral, which is just a patch of prairie, some fence, and a tethering post. Close by is a mule barn, blacksmith shop, and wagon yard. The men stand at the corral, looking over a herd of rowdy mustangs as Bugger Red speaks, "The army is interested in saddle broncos that meet certain specifications. These Texas mustangs are the very best. This puts Laredo in the rodeo business."

Frank asks, "Is Saturday the only day you break the mustangs?"

"No, some enterprising impresario hit on the idea of breaking the broncos on Saturday and Sunday, which draws a crowd of spectators. The spectators pay a token admission for a good location to park their carriages. They can also buy lemonade, beer, and tamales."

While Bugger speaks, the vendors hawk their wares, helping folks park their carriages. Bugger Red chews on a cigar, turns away, and talks with Ray Chadwick and McGhee, as a black cowboy nicknamed "Smokey" crosses the corral and leans against the fence. The men all gather around Smokey and continue to talk among themselves, occasionally looking Benny's way who has climbed to the top rail of the corral. Bugger winks at Smokey.

"Got any killer broncos you're having trouble with, Smokey?"

"Yeah, we got an outlaw horse I been saving for you. He threw me so high—it took me a week to come back down."

Bugger motions toward Benny. "Bring that outlaw out here and give it a good look at Ben Lester Binion."

Smokey ropes a big black thoroughbred with a white blaze and three white stocking feet. Rodeo fans scatter when the horse crashes through the corral fence, dragging Smokey behind him. The crowd quickly gathers. Benny helps the wranglers bring the large black horse under control. Bugger bows to Benny and takes hold of the bridle and motions for Benny to mount the outlaw horse. Frank shakes his head in disbelief as Benny gives his hat a tug and grins. Chadwick looks at Bobby McGhee and winks. Bugger Red turns to the crowd.

"This here is Ben Lester Binion from Pilot Grove, Texas, ain't a horse been born he can't ride."

Benny approaches the big black horse, seemingly careless of the outlaw's wild lunges and flying hoofs. He places a hand on the black's shoulder. He nods to the wranglers and mounts the horse with one quick movement. For a moment, the animal stands still and sulks. Benny puts his thumbs in his suspenders and grins at the crowd.

"Folks, this black outlaw horse has come all the way to Laredo to get a cowboy on his back—Eeeee haaaw, here we go."

Benny doesn't wait for the horse. He deliberately digs his thumb deep into the black horse's withers and swats him with his hat. Like a missile from a catapult, the black horse leaps high into the air. He hits the ground with all four legs straight, causing a sickening impact that would have crippled an ordinary bronc rider. The horse and Benny are hidden from the spectators by a cloud of dust as the big black horse sun fished then hog-rolled and pitched sideways.

When the black horse can finally be seen through the dust, Benny is still riding the outlaw like he's grown to him.

The crowd breaks into one giant enthusiastic cheer. Holding his hat high in the air, Smokey shouts, "My Lordy, it's a beautiful thing to see bronc riding at its best!"

By the time Benny parades the lathered horse around the corral, there's not a person in the crowd who isn't cheering. He slides from the outlaw horse and pats its neck. The crowd pours into the corral, trying to get close and shake Benny's hand.

Later that night in the Laredo pool hall, Bugger Red is soundly defeating Benny in a game of pool as he swaggers, cursing freely. Benny receives some sage advice as Bugger aligns his shots and jokes about each shot and his luck.

Chewing on a unlit cigar, "Horses is like humans. The mean ones you gotta command and handle tough—some you have to handle gently and sweet talk 'em—others can never be approached from the rear or they'll be out of sight and long gone never to return."

Bugger makes some sensational shots as he dances and struts around the pool table, twirling his cue stick like a baton. If he missed a shot, Bugger would always say, "Remind me to put an extra dollar in the collection plate next Sunday morning." He stands aside as Benny lines up on his shot and rattles on. "Take good care of your mamma and daddy. Always be honest—it pays in the long run. Have all the fun you can while you're alive—because when you're dead, you're dead for a long time."

Lining up for a corner pocket shot, Benny says, "Bugger, I'll try to remember all your good advice."

Early the next morning, Benny watches yearling calves mill about the Laredo stock pens. He soon mastered the art of calf roping. He was a fast learner. It was a pleasure to watch him work with the rope. Frank and a few cowhands watch Benny work his cutting horse. Benny sizes a loop, making it smaller or larger with just one hand, while holding his horse's reins in the other hand.

He ropes a calf by its back feet and drags it to the branding fire. As cowhands hold the calf, he dismounts and takes the red-hot iron from the fire and deftly applies the iron, leaving a perfect brand.

Longhorn cattle are bunched in one end of the corral. Ray Chadwick, on horseback, crowds a longhorn on the run as Benny jumps from his horse and bulldogs the steer. Bobby McGhee quickly ropes and ties the feet of the steer. Benny uses a saw to cut off the steer's horns close to the head, the proper way so the cattle can be loaded into boxcars at the railhead. He has learned everything there is to know about cattle, as well as treating them for pinkeye or screwworms.

PAPACHE VALDEZ

AFTER A HARD day's work, Benny and Frank sit at a table, beer bottles and empty plates shoved aside. Frank offers Benny a cigar and lights one for himself.

"Benny, I got a chance to make some serious money before I go back to El Paso. I want to cut you and the boys in on it."

"You said the magic word, Frank—you know I thrive on cash. Ieeee."

Frank lowers his voice, leaning close to Benny. "There is a badass Mexican by the name of Papache Valdez, he wants to cut a deal. Valdez has a ranch just outside of Saltillo. The bastard ran guns to a bunch of Villa's bandits—now he deals in everything, from dope and whiskey to women and rustling cattle. He wants me to take a herd of stolen Texas cattle to a buyer in Catulla."

"You know you can count on me, Frank."

The next morning, Benny and the boys herd cattle into a holding pen at a railroad siding. Frank negotiates with a cattle buyer. Papers are signed and money changes hands as the last of the cattle are driven from the holding pens and into a line of waiting cattle cars.

That night, Benny, Frank, Bobby McGhee, Ray Chadwick, and Smokey are drinking and celebrating. Frank hands each man a bulging envelope stuffed with money. "I want you boys to get the hell out of town—go home, shack up, whatever you need to do to get out of sight. Benny, I want you to stay in Laredo with me. I am going to tell Papache that Mexican bandits stole his cattle." The men roar with laughter and slap each other on the back as they leave the table. Frank and Benny remain. "I'm going to call for a meeting, supposedly to pay Papache."

"How do I fit in, Frank?"

"Papache will expect to be paid. Instead, I'm gonna kill him—I want you to watch my back."

Grinning, Benny says, "I got no problem with that."

Just after sunset, the next night as Frank and Benny leave the hotel, Benny is carrying a Winchester model '74 lever-action repeating rifle under a rain slicker at Frank's side.

About halfway across the railroad bridge over the Rio Grande, they approach the specified meeting place on the Mexican side of the river. There is a large empty box beside the railroad track. Benny uses the box to take rest with his Winchester as he hunkers down in the shadows. A mist is rising from the river. Benny watches over the sights of his rifle as Frank walks on across the bridge and into Mexico. The freight yard lights on the Mexican side produce enough light so that Benny has a clear field of fire. A couple of boxcars stand on a sidetrack only a few yards from the appointed place for the rendezvous. Papache and two of his henchmen step from the shadows. Benny sees Frank point to the boxcars on the siding. When Papache turns toward the boxcars, Frank draws his pistol and shoots Papache twice in the head.

Papache's knees buckle and he falls to the ground. Frank jumps to one side as gunfire breaks out from the top of the boxcars. Papache's two cohorts are caught in a field of withering gunfire.

Frank goes to Papache's body, un-holsters Papache's pistol, and fires it twice into the air, then throws it on the ground. Benny recognizes Frank's friends, two Texas Rangers, as they climb down from the boxcars, and he lets the hammer down on the Winchester—it's all over.

THE BIRTH OF TEXAS HOLD'EM

BENNY CHUCKLES IN his sleep as he recalls the birth of *Texas Hold'em* and we hear Bobby McGhee speak. Bobby was a ranch hand working on Frank Bass's "Hid Away Ranch," a safe harbor for stolen cattle and men on the run. Benny had been in a shooting scrape in El Paso and Frank Bass, ex–Texas Ranger and El Paso town marshal, was, for a while, Benny's mentor.

Bobby told the following story. "The boys played poker by the light of a coal oil lantern, which hung from the ceiling of the kitchen in a ranch bunkhouse. The hired hands changed from time to time as they left the ranch or were sometimes restrained by the law.

"Benny had established himself as the leader and enforcer of poker playing and his leadership was never challenged. Benny was a careful drinker and the life he had led in Pilot Grove growing up watching poker games in the mule barn and around campfires had sharpened the young man's mind.

"During those early years, Benny had learned to 'count

cards' a prerequisite for poker and a definite advantage for the player who learns."

Bobby McGee continued, "I've always been a fair hand at poker, but I never learned to read Benny's game. He played fast and loose. It was hard to believe some of the reckless hands he drew to. I've seen him raise twenty dollars with a pair of fours. He was always ready to draw to an inside straight and filled it so many times. I will never forget the night that Benny filled not one, but two inside straights while coming from behind and challenging Sam Evans.

"Frank Bass had introduced Sam to the boys earlier in the day. Benny took a shine to him 'cause earlier that week Sam had killed a federal in Cadillos. The boys joked and said it sort of made Benny and Sam brothers under the skin 'cause Benny just last month had put three holes in a federal in a gunfight in a Mexican whorehouse in Juarez and Frank Bass had broke Benny out of a Mexican jail and put him to work on his Hid Away Ranch.

"We all liked Sam right away, but he was sort of crazy. You had to tread lightly. He was a big-chested, black-bearded brute of a man. Rumor had it that he had killed a couple of men in Dallas while holding up a streetcar.

"That night in the bunkhouse kitchen, the whiskey and the cards came out, the newcomer, Sam Evans, and the other hands took a seat to see how the cards would run. Benny had created a set of rules that everyone thought was a pretty good idea. Since cheating was a common practice and we all knew it, Benny showed us a flat method of dealing, meaning the cards were dealt from the tabletop not held in the dealer's hand. This method eliminated dealing seconds or dealing from the bottom of the deck. Benny further insisted that a designated dealer deal the entire game instead of passing the deal. These rules worked real good and put any newcomer to the game at ease.

"We were all drinking our whiskey straight, except Chappy

the Mexican cook, he was drinking panther milk, a mixture of mescal, milk, and sugar. His stomach had been hurting him. None of the pots had amounted to anything, till about an hour into the game, when suddenly, we were looking at a pot worth more than a hundred dollars. Benny took the pot. He drew to a straight open at both ends. Sam cursed and pounded the table with both hands he held three jacks, two in the hole and one showing. Benny grinned at Sam and said, 'Tough one to lose, Sam. But hell, ain't they all?'

"Although Benny was red-eyed, you'd never known he had put down as much whiskey as Sam. Benny could hold his liquor. I don't ever remember it tangling his feet or making his speech slurred.

"Sam was so steamed he wouldn't even look at Benny. I was the designated dealer and Sam growled at me, 'Deal the damn cards, Bobby!' About half an hour later, Benny hit Sam again. Benny filled a straight flush to beat Sam's full house, aces over tens, and took over two hundred dollars off the table.

"Sam shoved his chair back from the table with a loud scrape, reaching for a meat cleaver on the kitchen stove. 'Goddamnit! I've never seen such luck of the draw!' and he started for Benny. Ray Chadwick looked at me and winked as he ducked under his bunk and came out with a sawed-off ten-gauge shotgun. As Sam rushed Benny with the meat cleaver drawn back, Benny stepped into Sam and hit him square between the eyes. At the same time, Chadwick fired into the ceiling just as Sam got hit.

"Sam went down amid plaster and dust from a huge hole in the ceiling. He lay still as a stone, his eyes closed. Chappy stepped inside from taking a piss and thought Sam had been shot. Sam let out a low groan, sat up, and put his hands to his face. He looked all around, like he wasn't sure if he was dead or alive. Chappy pointed at Sam and said, 'My god, it's Lazarus come back from the dead.' Not one of us could keep from laughing, not even Sam, he was so glad to find out he was not dead.

"Frank Bass burst into the room, his revolver drawn. Surveying the room, he holstered his gun. We made room for Frank at the table, but there was a problem. This brought the number of players to eight. Sam complained, 'There ain't enough cards in the deck to play our favorite game seven-card stud.'

"Benny responded there is a game the men at Pilot Grove played called *Pilot Grove Hold'em*, as many as ten may play, with just one deck of cards. We listened as Benny dealt a hand and explained, 'It's a lot like seven-card stud, each player gets two hole cards.' Benny grinned as he dealt and looked at each man. 'The betting begins here. Now the next three cards are dealt faceup and are called the flop.'

"As Benny dealt the three cards faceup, he explained, "You are using your two hole cards and the flop as your hand. You also know that each player is using the three cards in the flop as a part of his hand. After the betting on these five cards, when the dealer declares the pot is right, another card is dealt faceup in the middle of the table beside the flop called *Fourth Street.*

"'After betting on the *fourth street card* and the pot is right, the final and seventh card is dealt called the *river card*. You now have two hole cards and five cards up in the middle of the table, a total of seven to make your hand.

"'A player may declare that he is going *all-in* by betting his entire stack of chips on the turn of any card. Any player that does not match this bet must drop out and loses whatever he has put in the pot.'

"Surveying the hand he had dealt, Benny explained, 'Even with ten players, you have used a total of twenty hole cards and only five cards in the middle of the table makes your deck go a long way.'

"After playing Benny's *Pilot Grove Hold'em,* anything else

seemed boring. The rule of going all-in added luster to the game of poker and that's all we played from then on, but we did change the name of the game to *Texas Hold'em*."

BENNY COMES TO DALLAS

Thursday, October 18, 1923, morning's first light finds Frank and Benny, who has a beautiful saddle swung over his shoulder. They stand beside a boxcar as Frank's friend Shack unlocks the boxcar door. Frank explains, "Those two Texas Rangers are on my payroll. Just remember, Benny, some of the best crooks you can hire will be lawmen." Benny, Frank, and Shack all laugh.

Frank hands Benny a sealed white envelope. "When you get to Dallas, Benny, I want you to give this envelope to Joe Civello— he's the Dallas Mafia boss. His office is in a two-story gray brick building with a white balcony in the marketplace." The Shack turns and walks away toward the panting locomotive as Benny and Frank shake hands. Benny throws his saddle into the boxcar and then hoists himself up in as the train whistles twice and chugs away.Fourteen hours later, the locomotive pulling a string of freight cars enters the Dallas freight yards. The year is 1923, the shank of the Roaring Twenties, the same year Al Capone came to Chicago and organized crime has gained momentum since the passing of the Volstead Act, prohibiting the sale of alcoholic beverages. An elite Mafia organization headed by Joe Civello holds Dallas, Texas, in an iron-clad grip of illegal manufacturing and distribution of booze. As Benny's freight train grinds to a halt, a door on the boxcar opens. Benny swings to the ground and reaches back inside for his saddle, swings it over his shoulder, and starts down the track toward the bright lights of downtown Dallas. He hears a commanding voice from behind. "Does that saddle belong to you, cowboy?" Benny puts the saddle down and turns to face Bill Decker, who is only a few years older than Benny, five foot eleven inches tall, one hundred and seventy pounds, wearing leather jacket and a dark brown fedora, Decker patting his hand with a billy club.Benny grins good-naturedly and says, "The saddle is mine, sir. My name is Ben Lester Binion and I'm from Pilot Grove, Texas. I want us to be friends."

The light of a passing train shines on Decker's face. He waits for the noise of the locomotive to pass. "I'm Bill Decker, Dallas County Sheriff's Office. Mr. Binion, do you have a bill of sale for that saddle?"

Benny's determined blue eyes meet the intense stare of the lawman. "No papers, sir—but the saddle is mine, I bought it in El Paso from the Morales Leather Goods Company."

"If you don't have a bill of sale, Mr. Binion, you will have to come with me so we can get this sorted out."

Decker watches Benny closely, still patting his hand with his billy club. "Do you have a problem with that?"

Benny picks up his saddle. "No, sir, Mr. Decker. Like I said earlier, I want us to be friends."

The two men walk toward the lights of the county jail, which can be seen from the freight yards. Decker leads Benny to the desk sergeant, a taciturn and sour-faced man. "What have we got here, Decker?"

"This is Ben Lester Binion—he's from Pilot Grove. We're not

booking him—just checking him in for holdover for possible stolen property."

The chief jailor Floyd Lyons, a tall good-natured blond man smoking a pipe, approaches. "Mr. Binion, have you had supper yet?"

"I'm sure proud you asked. I'm so hungry I could eat the south end of a northbound mule."

"Follow me, Mr. Binion. The regulars have been fed, but we'll see what's left."

Next morning, Bill Decker is standing at Benny's cell as he clinks a mug of steaming coffee against the cell bars. Benny sits up rubbing the sleep from his eyes. "How about some breakfast, Benny. It won't be anything fancy, but it will be hot and plenty of it."

"That sounds great, Mr. Decker."

Benny and Decker take a seat at a table as two trustees serve up food from a steaming stainless steel serving table, inmates waiting in line. An occasional hearty burst of male laughter can be heard over the breakfast noise. Decker reads from a legal-size paper on a clipboard. "We checked with El Paso. No one reported a missing saddle. Seems you got into a few scrapes—gambling and fighting and some petty theft—but nothing you couldn't handle."A trustee puts food on the table and the two men eat their breakfast. Finishing first, Decker lights a cigarette and studies Benny through the cigarette smoke. "Ben Lester, you're no choirboy, but you came away from El Paso clean. When was the last time you talked to your family in Pilot Grove?"

Benny looks up from his plate. "Mr. Decker, I left home four years ago. I'm anxious to get back to Pilot Grove and see my folks." Benny reaches for the last biscuit and wipes his plate with it.

"Ben Lester, do you know how to use a telephone?"

Benny shakes his head no. "Mr. Decker, my friends call me Benny, and I want us to be friends."

"OK, Benny. We have a telephone in the sheriff's office. You are not being held, so before you go, I'll be glad to help you put a call through to your folks."

"Thanks, Mr. Decker, my folks don't have a phone, but my uncle Eddie does at his syrup mill, and I'd sure like to talk with him."

The two men leave the jail kitchen and take the elevator to the ground floor. No one is in the sheriff's office and Decker places the phone call, then he hands the phone to Benny, and while Benny talks, Decker leaves.

On the second floor, a sign over the door reads Property Room. The clerk, a friendly elderly graying man retrieves Benny's saddle. "That's a fine-lookin' saddle. I was kinda hoping you'd leave it with me, Benny."

Benny throws the saddle over his shoulder. "Thank you, sir. But I wouldn't leave without my saddle."Benny returns to the first floor and the desk sergeant, his saddle swung over his shoulder. "Sir, how do I get to the Dallas fish and produce market?"

"Four blocks east on Houston Street, take a left turn and you're there."

As Benny steps into the street, the morning is crisp and clear. He walks past the Red Courthouse and downtown buildings.

JOE CIVELLO, DALLAS MAFIA DON

IN THE MARKETPLACE, there is a carnival atmosphere of bustling activity, produce is being unloaded from wagons and displayed in stalls. Vendors shout, hawking their wares. A train whistles nearby; a mule bray, horse's hoofs clatter against the pavement, and a roster can be heard crowing over the hubbub of laughter and muted conversations. A sign hangs over the street that reads Winem Hotel. Two attractive young ladies hang over the hotel balcony. "Hey, cowboy, bring your saddle up here and we'll give you a ride you'll never forget." Recognizing the girls as sporting ladies, Benny puts his saddle down, tips his hat, and blows them a kiss. "Perhaps tomorrow—I'm going to visit my sick mother." The ladies burst into laughter and blow kisses back to Benny.

HE STOPS IN front of a building painted gray. A white New Orleans–type ironwork balcony extends from the east side. A neatly painted sign on the sparkling glass window reads JOE CIVELLO & SONS' Dallas Fish & Produce Company. Inside the building, Benny is greeted by Jeffrey, a smiling Mexican, standing behind a white glass display case with scales on the countertop. The display case is full of filleted fish, shrimp, and oysters packed in ice. Jeffrey wipes his hands on his white apron. "What can I do for you, my friend?"

Benny puts his saddle down. I'm looking for a Mr. Joe Civello. Jeffrey turns toward the rear of the store and calls, "Christina, come here." A young Mexican girl comes from an office. "Yes, Papa?" Jeffrey, gesturing, says, "Go upstairs and tell Mr. Civello there is a man here to see him."Christina pauses, looking at Benny. "He always asks me who is here to see him. Who may I say is calling?"

"Tell Mr. Civello a friend of Frank Bass in El Paso is here to deliver an envelope."She hurries up the stairs at the rear of the room and soon returns. "Mr. Civello will be pleased to see you. He asks that you come up to his office."

Benny, still carrying his saddle, climbs the stairs. At the top of the stairs, a hallway extends the length of the building. To his left are closed doors. To the right, a heavy wooden door with a massive ornate brass lock stands open. A voice from within says, "Come in—I've been expecting you, Mr. Binion." Benny enters a large impressive office.

Joe Civello, a man of small stature, handsome, tastefully dressed in a tailored suit, is seated behind a massive beautifully carved desk, which centers a Persian rug. The room opens onto a balcony with a table and chairs overlooking the activity of the market below. Civello rises to greet Benny and grips Benny's hand firmly, looking directly into his blue eyes. Civello runs his hand over the intricate leather tooling of the saddle. Smiling at Benny, he reveals a perfect set of teeth that add to the charisma of his angular face.

"My sixth sense tells me that I am looking at a man with the heart and soul of a true mafioso—What a beautiful saddle."

"Thank you, Mr. Civello, I bought it in Laredo."

"May I?" Civello lifts the saddle from Benny's shoulder.

"Let's set it here, just inside the door, so you can keep an eye on it while we talk."

"Mr. Civello, Frank Bass asked me to deliver this envelope to you."

Civello takes the envelope, lays it on his desk, and turns back to Benny. "I'm so glad you are here, Mr. Binion."

"My friends call me Benny, Mr. Civello—I want us to be friends."

"All right, Benny, have a seat while I open Frank's envelope." He uses an ornate jewel-handled knife to open the envelope and reads the message, then puts it back in the envelope. "Benny, will you have lunch with me while we talk? Christina will set up the table for us on the balcony and we can watch the activity in the market below as we eat."

"I'm always ready to eat, Mr. Civello."

Chuckling, Civello rings a small silver bell on his desk. "Benny, Frank Bass speaks highly of you. His cryptic message makes you eligible to become a Mafia candidate. After a year of apprenticeship, you may then become a soldier. When this happens, you will have your foot on the first rung of a ladder that can carry you to great wealth."

"I'm always interested in making money, Mr. Civello."

Christina enters and places a tray with a wine bottle and glasses on the desk then leaves. Civello opens the wine and samples it, then pours a glass for Benny and himself. Holding his glass high and looking at Benny, "Here is to long life and enough money to enjoy it. Salude." As Civello sips his wine, he continues, "Should you choose to accept this opportunity, Frank will receive a gratuity for recommending you. But first—a few questions—I spoke with Frank on the phone, and he explained that he was dismantling his cattle operation for a while—the Laredo market has become very volatile." Pausing, Civello pours another glass of wine for the two of them.

"Tell me how you met Frank, Benny."

"I heard a lot of bad stories about Frank before I met him.

I tried to avoid him, but we wound up meeting head-on and I damn near drew on him. I realize now, that's when we really got to know each other." Civello dips the tip of his cigar in his wine glass and smiles as he listens with great interest. Benny continues, "Later on, Frank saved my life when he busted me out of a Mexican jail in Juarez. We became good friends that night—I figure I owe him my life, and then Frank asked me to back his play while he disposed of a badass Mexican. I did back his play and I learned a lot from Frank."Christina returns and sets a table. Stepping back into Civello's office, she places a bowl of black olives in front of him. Civello takes two olives and pushes the bowl toward Benny. "Try these olives with the wine, Benny." Benny nods and drains his glass.

"When I was a small boy in Sicily, I used to eat the olives right out of my father's barrels as I listened to the men talk. In order to give you light, so you may make a decision, I will tell you about my father and the old country. Perhaps it will be helpful to you to draw a parallel between our two countries. Sicily was first invaded by the Moors, then the French, the Romans, and the Spanish. She was often occupied, but never conquered." Civello pours more wine for Benny.

"One of my favorite stories is of a great feast given the Roman generals after the invasion. The Sicilians placed poison in their food and all the generals died. The people were good citizens by day, but conspired to have justice at night. Many throats of the occupying armies were cut at night while they slept. Lip service was given to the laws of the land, but it was Sicilian justice and revenge that ruled, not the armies of occupation."

Civello takes more olives and refills his wineglass. "My father was a man who lived by strict rules of his own. His protocol made him respected for all his life. His principles generated extraordinary fear, which was the basis of his power. A chief tenet of that protocol was complete lack of mercy—while I ate my father's black olives—I listened and learned well."Christina returns with a large bowl of green salad, some cheese, and crisp bread. Benny follows Civello to the table on the balcony. The sky is clear and the weather is crisp with a slight breeze. The table gives the men the vantage of a view of the activities in the marketplace below. As Civello tucks a napkin into his shirt, he continues.

"When your country was invaded and under the rule of a conquering army, which enforced the laws of the northern carpetbaggers and the hated Texas police, you remember how John Wesley Hardin and your Bobby Lee dealt with the Texas police and carpetbaggers? I make this comparison. In Sicily, after centuries of occupation, there was a much-better organized national effort."Christina brings plates of shrimp scampi accompanied by spaghetti. Plunging two forks deep into the spaghetti, Civello puts a mound of pasta on Benny's plate. After serving himself, he uses a large spoon and his fork to roll the spaghetti into a ball and then pierces one of the succulent shrimp with his fork. Amused, he watches Benny attempt to emulate him. "Keep trying, Benny—you will master the Italian art of eating spaghetti yet." Civello smiles as he hears Benny say, "I'm fascinated with your story of Sicilian history and this food is great."

"Sicily is a dry, arid country and water is a scarce commodity. The dons, who controlled the water, extracted their toll from other farmers. The government attempted to build dams that would provide the much-needed water, but the powerful water barons fought the government, both politically and with terrorism. Today, in Sicily, those same dons still control the country's water."

"Your government has provided our Dallas organization with a tremendous opportunity to become wealthy. Prohibition is a very unpopular law and few people care whether it is enforced or not."

"The Dallas breweries, impounded and padlocked by the government, remain in business today. Every drop of impounded alcohol has been sold out the back door. The Dallas police and politicians continue to look the other way with their hand out. This ridiculous law enables us to sell the alcohol at a higher price."

Christina returns to serve espresso and a plate of Italian pastries. Civello sips his espresso and continues.

"Today, I am able to apply those same principles to the manufacture and sale of whiskey and beer that my forefathers applied to the control of water in Sicily. Small independent stills continue to pop up, and I am constantly attempting to persuade them to comply with our system. Of course, there are concessions to other men's self-interests—that is only reasonable. But if all else fails, threats or acts of punishment that might lead to retaliation are not used—the problem is simply banished from the face of the earth—amaretto men that are dead tell no tales."

A KNIFE FIGHT IN THE DALLAS MARKETPLACE

IN THE MARKETPLACE below Civello's balcony, Tom Stewart, a Grayson county farmer, short, stocky, middle-aged, wearing striped overalls and a sweat-stained straw hat, drives his wagon into the market. A large black dog sits obediently at his side. Sacks of pecans fill the wagon, which is pulled by two mules. Tom Stewart parks his wagon and waits for the produce buyer to grade his pecans.

A yellow bitch dog in heat, followed by a pack of snarling, snapping male dogs, runs through the market. The big black dog leaps from the seat. Tom shouts, "Buster! Buster! Come back here!"

Buster ignores his master and chases after the pack of dogs following the yellow bitch dog.

A large brindle pit bull challenges Buster. As the fight evolves, Rocky, the pit bull, gets a strangle hold on Buster's throat. Unable to shake the pit bull loose, Buster falls to the ground.

Tom leaps from the wagon and cautiously approaches the growling and snapping dogs. He manages to get his hand on Rocky's collar, but the pit bull won't release its grip on Buster's throat. Tom kicks the pit bull with all his might, but to no avail. He is about to kick the pit bull again when Frank Bolding, a huge black man with a badly scarred face, grabs Tom's collar and pulls him back. Tom pulls a knife from his pocket and slashes at Frank.

Civello and Benny hear the commotion and rush to the balcony rail.

"Christina, bring me my binoculars!"

The two men circle each other with knives. Frank Bolding cuts Tom's suspender. Within a few moments, the other suspender is cut and the crowd laughs as Tom tries to hold up his overalls and fight at the same time. Frank Bolding grabs hold of Tom's knife hand, reaches around the smaller man, and viciously twists his knife between Tom's ribs. The fight that at first was comical has now turned ugly. A woman's voice from the crowd screams, "Someone stop the fight, he is going to kill that man!"

The tenacious pit bull, still gripping Buster's throat, has punctured a jugular vein. Blood saturates the ground. Buster makes one last effort to survive. Frank Bolding moves behind Tom who is weak and staggering. Oblivious to the dogs, the onlookers watch in horror as Frank Bolding pulls Tom's head back and cuts his throat. A spray of blood reflects in the afternoon sun as the carotid artery is severed. Releasing Tom, Frank Bolding moves in front of Tom.

"Sorry damn white trash—don't come to my market, kick my dog, and pull your puny knife on me." Tom collapses and lies writhing in agony as Frank savagely kicks the dying man. In horror, women cover their faces as the crowd hisses and murmurs its disapproval.

Putting the binoculars down, and without looking at Benny,

"The black man is Frank Bolding, one of our soldiers. That is not the first man he has killed. It's a cruel world out there."

Benny feels a cold rush of rage having witnessed a senseless killing and thinks to himself, "It's not my place to comment one way or the other, but I'll always have my pistol handy around Frank Bolding."

FLIP YA DOUBLE OR NOTHING

L ATER THAT EVENING, Benny walks the few blocks to the Texas Electric Railway Station. He puts his saddle down at the ticket window tended by a ticket clerk, an old man with glasses sitting hunched over in his booth.

"I need a round-trip ticket to Van Alstyne."

The ticket clerk looks at a clipboard. "That will be seventy cents, young feller."

Benny pays the clerk, takes his ticket, and picks up his saddle and takes a seat in the station room to wait for the trolley.

Once aboard and traveling home, Benny looks out the window and watches for Van Alstyne to come into view. Finally the trolley comes to a halt. Benny picks up his saddle and swings to the ground. He heads down the street to Cockers' Livery Stable; Bud Cocker, a stocky man with a butch haircut, is in the tack room mending harness. Benny slips up behind Bud, cups his hands, and shouts in Bud's ear, "What's the best horse you got in your string, mister?"Bud looks around startled. "Ben Lester Binion—where ya been. Hell, I thought the hogs had ate you." Benny drops his saddle, grabs Bud, and the two men grapple in a circle, laughing and grunting like a couple of young mules. The horseplay over, Bud sits down, putting his feet up on his desk. Benny sits on a bench. "I see your saddle, Benny, where's your horse?"

"That's why I came to see you, Bud. What's the best horse you got in your string?" Bud reaches in his pocket and takes out a plug of tobacco, cuts himself a chew, and offers some to Benny, who shakes his head no.

"I got a big black Tennessee Walker."

"Let's take a look at the big hay burner."

Benny follows Bud into the stables. Bud unlatches a door and leads the black Tennessee Walker out. Knowing full well that is the horse he wants, Benny says, "He's all right—what else you got, Bud?"

"I got a buckskin horse that's a little old, but he's smart."

Benny pauses as if considering the buckskin. "What are you asking for the Tennessee Walker?"

"Benny, I got three hundred in that horse. I been asking four hundred, but seeing as how we're kin and all—for you it would be three fifty."

"Let me put my saddle on him and I'll make you an offer."

Bud hands him a blanket. Benny puts the blanket and his saddle on the big horse, slips a bit into his mouth, tucks the horse's ears into the bridle, and buckles it in place. He runs his hand over the horse's neck as he leads the big Tennessee Walker outside. He talks softly as he strokes the horse's muzzle. "He hasn't been rode in a while, Ben Lester—he may be a little cranky." Benny takes a tug on his hat and mounts the big black horse with one quick move. The animal sulks, his ears laid back. He shouts, "Open the corral gate, Bud." Bud moves quickly to the gate. Benny gouges the horse with his thumb, kicking him in the flank at the same time. "Here we go, Bud!"

The big horse jumps straight into the air and comes down in a twist, straight-legged, then leaps straight forward, kicking its hind legs out. All the while, Benny holds a tight rein, pulling the animal's head to one side. When the black horse finally straightens out, Benny pulls his head so he can see the open corral gate. The animal bolts for the open gate as Benny kicks the horse in the flank and lets him have his head. "Eeeee Haaaaa!"Man and animal, moving in a cloud of dust, bolt by Bud through the corral gate. Bud grins—he knows he's made a sale. A few minutes later, Bud watches from inside the corral as Benny rides the horse back at an easy gate. "How old do you think he is, Bud?"

"Oh hell, Benny—I'd say he'd just got growed, maybe a little past two years. He's one of the prettiest blacks we've had come through here—I thought about you when I first saw him."

"Give me a cut off that wad of tobacco you got in your pocket." Bud hands him the tobacco. Benny cuts a plug and stuffs it in his mouth, then walks over to the horse, takes hold of the bridle, and lifts the horse's muzzle to examine his teeth. "Bud, I'd say he's closer to four than two—but three fifty is fair enough. I'll pay your price."

With his back to Bud, Benny counts out the three hundred and fifty dollars and then pushes the remaining roll deep into his pocket. As he turns back to Bud, he holds the money out to him, at the same time offering, "Flip ya double or nothing?"

Bud pauses and thinks for a moment. "You got the other three fifty on you?"

"Sure do, Bud."

"I flip the coin and it lands in the dirt?"

"That sounds fair enough—I'll call it while it's in the air."

Benny reaches in his pocket and hands Bud a silver dollar. Bud spits in his hand, takes the coin and rubs it, then holds it up to his lips and whispers, "You ready, Ben Lester?"

"Let her rip, Bud!"

The dollar arches high into the sunlight.

Benny calls out, "Tails!"

The coin hits the coral dust close to Bud's feet.

"What does the eagle say, Bud?" Bud stares at the coin for a moment. "Ben Lester Binion, you're the luckiest bastard that ever pulled on a pair of boots—take your damn horse and git out of here!"

LONNIE LEANS THE SHOTGUN AGAINST THE PORCH RAIL

BENNY AND THE big black horse travel at an easy gate with the late-afternoon sun at their back. An occasional dog challenges them as they travel a country road moving ever closer to the Binion plantation and home. The sun dips below the horizon and only the pink twilight remains. Benny turns his big black horse into a lane through a canopy of pecan trees leading to a two-story freshly painted white-framed house. The Binion hounds come out to challenge the stranger on horseback. The guineas perched on their roost set up a clamor, sounding the alarm of an intruder. Lonnie and Jack step from the light of the family home to the porch. Lonnie has a shotgun cradled in his arms as he peers into the twilight. Benny doesn't call out, but dismounts and leads his horse toward the porch.

The light is dim and Lonnie squints his eyes clouded with age, does not recognize the stranger. Jack, however, does. Without a word, he springs from the porch and runs full force, throwing himself at Benny in a flying tackle. The two men tumble to the ground. The family dogs bark and join in the horseplay as Benny overpowers Jack.

"Eeeeee! Gotcha now, little brother!"Lonnie leans the shotgun against the porch rail and embraces his two sons, not saying a word, just holding them tight. Benny's fourteen-year-old sister, Dorothy, steps onto the porch, recognizes Benny, and turns back toward the house. Excited, Dorothy calls out, "Mama—it's Ben Lester—he's home!" Benny rushes to his mother as she comes out onto the porch and embraces her, then hugs Dorothy. "You're getting all growed up and pretty as a picture, sis."

Lonnie moves close to Benny. "They've been cooking for you all day, Ben Lester." Jack takes the reins of the Tennessee Walker, talking to him gently, and leads him toward the barn.A dining room table is loaded down with fried chicken and food of every description and, of course, a can of Uncle Eddy's sorghum syrup. Benny tells about his adventures as the family listens spellbound. After the meal, Dorothy brings in a birthday cake with candles and they all sing happy birthday to Benny.

BENNY GOES TO WORK FOR
THE DALLAS MAFIA DON

THE NEXT AFTERNOON, Benny finds a sign across the roof of a building on Singleton in Dallas that reads "Ray's Lumber and Hardware." Benny enters the store. One wall of the store is lined with every type of rifle and shotgun imaginable. A display case contains numerous types of pistols. Ray Brantley, a good-natured young man, talks with a customer while Benny admires the many weapons. Ray turns to assists Benny in the selection of two .45 automatics, a .38 revolver with an ankle holster with cloth cases for each weapon. He also buys a Winchester model 12 pump shotgun and a trunk to carry the newly acquired weapons and ammunition.Benny takes the shotgun to the gunsmith on the second floor and instructs the gunsmith, Jim, a graying older man, of the modifications he wants to make the weapon a whippet. As Benny watches and instructs, the gunsmith cuts off all but five inches of the barrel and the stock is cut down to a pistol grip. A latch screw is inserted into the end of the remaining stock.

Finishing the modifications, Jim hands the shotgun to Benny and says, "There is your whippet, Mr. Binion, you can whip that out from under your coat as if by magic and take control of almost any situation." Both men laugh as Benny puts the deadly weapon in a custom-built leather case that looks much like a musical instrument container.A street car stops downtown Dallas in front of a four-story red brick hotel. The sign reads Oriental Hotel. The building has a turret at one corner. Benny steps down from the street car and enters the opulent hotel lobby with red carpeting. The furniture and ornate picture frames washed in gold, carrying the trunk on his shoulder.He stops at the front desk and arranges for a room. A young bellhop grunts as he lifts the trunk onto a dolly and leads Benny up the stairs to his room. Benny tips the bellhop, and when the door is closed, he makes sure it's locked. He opens the trunk and takes out the shotgun. Benny ties a piece of rawhide in a loop, passing it through the latch screw on the butt of the shotgun. He sticks his arm through the loop and lets the shotgun hang to his side, then puts his coat on over the shotgun. Facing the mirror, he dips his right shoulder slightly forward, pulling his coat back with his left hand. The shotgun swings forward into his right hand; satisfied, he smiles at himself in the mirror and snaps the trigger. Laughing, he pumps the shotgun and shouts, "Boom! Boom! Boom!"

Having his arsenal in a safe place, Benny calls on Joe Civello, the Dallas Mafia don. When Benny enters his office, Civello rises from his desk and comes around to shake Benny's hand and pours him a glass of wine and one for himself, and the men sit down.

"Benny, have you reached a decision?"

"Yes, sir. I have decided to help you with your plan."

Civello holds a humidor toward Benny. Benny takes a cigar and the two men light up. "There is a modest home on Pocahontas Street, not far from here. It will be your lodging and your charge. Our whiskey is warehoused in a large garage at the rear of the house."

"You want me to guard and distribute the whiskey at the warehouse?"

Nodding, Civello says, "That is correct. We do not pay our soldiers a wage. However, you will be paid a commission determined by the cash flow from the sale of the whiskey." After answering Benny's questions, Civello leads the way as they walk a few blocks to the intersection of Akard and then to the Ristorante Vesuvio. They enter through an ornate plate glass door. Joe Ianni, a short smiling man wearing a tomato-stained apron, hurries to greet Civello and Benny. Joe Ianni and Benny shake hands. "My friends call me Vick, Mr. Binion. Come this way. Some friends of mine have heard of you and are anxious to meet you and hear your stories of El Paso."Joe Ianni leads Benny and Civello the length of the restaurant and up steps opposite the kitchen. At a landing at the top of the stairs is a heavy ornate door. Joe Ianni opens the door and stands aside to let Benny and Civello enter. Civello, rubbing his hands together, says, "I'm sure when I get to heaven, it will smell like this!"

A long table is centered with two huge bowls of spaghetti and various Italian dishes along with a variety of wines. Chairs scrape as the men around the table stand. Civello calls each man by name as Benny is introduced.

He meets Joe Campisi, Sam Campisi, Phillip Bosco, and James La Barba. The formalities over, the men reseat themselves. Civello directs Benny to the seat of honor at his right. Raising his wineglass, he says, "I propose a toast to our new soldier, Benny, who comes recommended by our good friend, Frank Bass, of El Paso." The men raise their glasses, saluting Benny.

"Now, let us eat the excellent food Vick has prepared— and drink his good wine." When the meal is finished, Joe Ianni passes a box of cigars. The men get comfortable as

Civello stands to speak. "For the benefit of our new soldier, Joe Campisi will depict the story of the Sicilian vespers."

Joe Campisi, a handsome tall man with dark hair, rises from his chair. "When the French under the Bourbon monarchy occupied Sicily, they were an unusually cruel army of occupation. Taking advantage of their power, the French took what was not theirs, with the arrogant sense that this was their right. As conquerors, they were brutal and inflicted pain and harm on the people. The relationship of the ordinary people with the French was one of sullen and smoldering resentment.

"One evening in Palermo, according to the story, a French soldier saw a beautiful girl accompanied by her mother on the way to vespers at a nearby church—the soldier felt it was his right as conqueror to take the young girl. He shoved the mother aside and dragged the girl into the shadows and proceeded to rape her—the mother ran through the streets screaming, 'Ma Fia Ma Fia'—meaning, 'My family, my family.' A crowd quickly gathered. Riots and insurrection broke out. Outright and general rebellion followed.

"More typical of Sicilian response was the action of the woman's young suitor. Humiliated, shamed, and outraged, he set out in his own private way to seek justice. He learned the name of the soldier who had raped his beloved sweetheart. He found the place where the soldier slept and cut his throat in the darkness of night." At this point, all the men stand and applaud. There is not a dry eye in the group. Joe Campisi bows from the waist. "Thank you for your heartfelt applause." The men take their seats and Joe Campisi continues. "To further enlighten our new soldier and friend, Ben Lester Binion, Joseph Civello will now give us the definition of the word *mafioso*."Civello rises and pauses for a long moment, his eyes resting on each man around the table. "A person can be mafioso in the sense of being a member of an organized clan, but at the same time, may not possess those qualities that are defined as mafioso. On the other hand, someone who has no affiliation whatsoever can be mafioso, just by being who he is. Gender has nothing to do with being mafioso—a beautiful proud woman can be mafioso. One does not even have to be a human being to exhibit mafioso qualities; a brave, fierce dog, a horse with a certain bearing, a lion—they can all be mafioso. Do not try to define the word too closely or you will miss its meaning—the quality is as mysterious as it is specific. It is surely in the soul—it is unmistakable—indefinable.

"A key component in all Mafia relationships is honor as defined by respect. It has nothing to do with affection. It is an acknowledgment of power and place—yours and someone else's. A mafioso is someone willing to acknowledge the power of, say, a judge, a legislator, a wealthy and influential businessman, or another Mafia leader—but the mafioso is not willing to tolerate an insult to his own honor in that relationship. The rape of a woman, or the abuse of the weak by a bully, is an act against honor that the mafioso cannot tolerate."

Civello smiles as he turns to Benny. "A word of advice for our new soldier—never fire at an officer of the law, submit peacefully and deny any wrongdoing. Such contingencies are foreseen and planned for. There are judges in Dallas who are stalwart in the defense of fair play. And one last word of advice—never date a woman who owns more than one cat."

With the last remark, the men roar with laughter. A drum beats and scantily clad dancing girls with tambourines dance into the room and the party begins.

A DALLAS KU KLUX KLAN LYNCH MOB MARCHES ON OLD RED

WHILE THE PARTY is taking place, a black 1923 La Salle four-door sedan pulls up in front of a jewelry store downtown Dallas on Elm Street. Three men get out and enter the store. They emerge with Tom Mott, a small but muscular man. A pillowcase has been placed over Mott's head and he is pushed into the backseat of the sedan. The car pulls away and fades into the night.

After driving south for a little more than an hour, the La Salle turns down a country lane and stops at a gate where a huge bonfire burns in a meadow surrounded by tall trees. A group of hooded Klansmen watch as an executioner wields a cat-o'-nine-tails, whipping a victim as a Klansman count the lashes. "Six—seven—"The next night in Sam Campisi's office, Tom Mott is told to take off his shirt.

Present are Joe Campisi, Joe Civello, Phillip Bosco, James La Barba. Mott turns his back to the men and reveals a mass of blood-caked lacerations. "Those Klan bastards tied me to a tree and whipped me with a cat-o'-nine-tails. The Klansman who whipped me—he and I were dating the same woman. The bastard told me to leave town or he'd put me on the spot." Warren Diamond interrupts. "Joe, I wanted you to see this for yourself and hear Mott's story. I am paying you people insurance to protect my people. The police won't do anything—most of the department belongs to the Klan anyway, and the chief is a grand dragon."Benny helps Mott ease himself back into a chair and then whirls around. Angry, Benny brings his clenched fist down hard on the table. He pauses to let his anger cool. "The unspoken truce between the Klan and Dallas gamblers has been broken, and with your permission, I'm gonna send a message to the Grand Cyclops himself, Hiram Wesley."

The men nod in agreement. Joe Civello, the Mafia don, steps forward, putting his hand on Tom Mott's shoulder. "Benny is our brave new soldier, let's listen to his plan."

"The word on the street—the Klan is mustering its forces to march on the county jail to lynch the Noel brothers. We can take advantage of the confusion that will be created and, with Mott's help, identify the Klansman who put him on the spot."

Warren Diamond speaks. "The Noel brothers—those are the two bastards who have been raping and butchering teenage girls and terrorizing Dallas. It's no wonder the Klan people are out for blood."Joe Civello says, "Yeah! They cut the breasts off their victims—when Decker caught 'em, a satchel filled with women's breasts was found in their car!"

Two days later just at dusk, the Dallas Power & Light Company can be seen from downtown Dallas. Two of the four smoke stacks emit a thin trail of wispy gray smoke. Inside the control room, Henry Clay, plant superintendent, a large, portly man in his late sixties, with KKK tattooed on the back of his left hand, sits at the power plant's main control panel. His assistant George Bean, a well-built young man, enters the area. Henry Clay looks at his watch.

"George, I have orders to black out downtown Dallas. Go downstairs and pull the toggle switch on grid 9!"

"But that would black out the entire downtown area, no streetlights, no traffic lights, no—"

Henry interrupts. "Let me make it simple for you. Either go downstairs and pull the switch on grid 9, or be fired!"

George turns on his heel and responds, "Yes, sir," as he leaves the control room.In front of the Majestic Theater, downtown Dallas on Elm Street, the Klan Drum & Bugle Corps, more than seven hundred strong, is mustered. They fidget as they await their cue to begin their march to the county jail. A stocky hooded midget dressed in full Klan regalia holding a burning taper runs through the Klan's ranks, lighting their torches. A color bearer, proudly holding the American flag, takes his place in front of a flaming cross. Across the street, light from the Majestic Theater marquee creates an eerie glow on the white sheets of the Klansmen. Suddenly, the entire downtown area is enveloped in darkness. The Klansmen cheer and bugles blare as the Klan steps off, their mission to raid the county jail and lynch the Noel brothers.

Eleven blocks away on Elm Street, the county jail lights go out. An emergency generator whines as it gathers speed. The jail lights flicker, then surge with power and come back on line as bright as ever.

In the distance, bugles punctuate a muffled drum cadence as the largest drum and bugle corps in the world is on the march. The Klan's torches and burning crosses cast a wavering, supernatural glow on the spectators lining the street.Fire trucks pull out of the fire station with red lights flashing and bells clanging. The trucks roar down Houston Street to the jail and form a barricade at the jail's only entrance.Benny and Tom Mott follow other bystanders who fall in with the Klansmen. Tom Mott spots his assailant, Shelby Morton, a large hooded Klansman who walks with a noticeable limp. He is in the main body of Klan ranks of the two thousand Klan force laying siege to the county jail at Elm and Houston streets. Tom Mott excitedly exclaims, "Mr. Binion, there he is—that's him—the man who used the lash on me."

Inside the county jail, the defiant chant of the Klan army can be heard. Bill Decker and Deputy Hickey Bright, midforties, stubby, with a combative nature, meet with Sheriff Skylar Marshall, tall, husky with sandy hair, wearing a brace of six-shooters. The Klan starts a chant, "Ku Klux Klan! Ku Klux Klan! Yesterday! Today! Tomorrow! Justice will be done! Lynch! Lynch! Lynch!" Decker shouts over the Klan noise, "Everything is in place, Sheriff; the skirmish line, fire trucks, and snipers. Four men with Thompson submachine guns are standing by."

"Good work, Decker—we're sure as hell not backing down to this Klan mob!"

Hickey Bright picks up a spittoon and spits a stream of tobacco juice into it and then wipes his mouth. "If we can just hold 'em off tonight, it'll be the first time they've ever been turned back—they've sure had their way up to now. Don't you think it's kind of worrisome that almost all our deputies are members?" Outside a block away, across the railroad tracks, at a Coca-Cola warehouse, the mob breaks through the gates and into the warehouse. Once inside, they grab wooden cases of empty Coke bottles and start carrying them toward the skirmish line of deputies who have cordoned off the county jail. Over the din of the mob, a group leader shouts, "Get two cases and stack 'em just in range of the deputies. When I signal, we'll rain Coke bottles on 'em! That'll soften 'em up—then we can rush 'em!"

The mob surges forward, pelting the deputies with Coke bottles and broken bricks. As the bottles fall to the ground, the deputies pick up the missiles and hurl them back at the mob.Decker mounts a fire truck; he takes a hose and nods to a nearby fireman. He aims a stream of water at the forefront of the mob, knocking several Klansmen off their feet.

Occasional pistol shots can be heard over the din of the battle. Klan snipers fire from adjacent buildings. Meanwhile, Decker continues to hold the mob at bay with powerful oscillating streams of water.A distraught, seemingly crazed woman, a shapely brunette, midthirties, runs screaming through a gap in the barricade. "Those bastards raped and murdered my sister. Why in heaven's name are you protecting them?" She then throws a Coke bottle at Decker, narrowly missing him. Glaring at Decker, she yells, "What if it were your sister or mother—would you still be protecting those butchers?"The mob forms and moves forward behind the crazed woman. Hesitating momentarily, Decker lets the woman get closer. Then he turns the hose on her full blast. It knocks her and the Klansmen around her to the ground. Two deputies rush outside the barricade and drag the screaming and kicking lady into the jail as Decker continues to hold the mob at bay with the fire hose.

A staccato of gunfire erupts from a nearby building. Decker's hat flies from his head and a trickle of blood appears above his eye. Wiping the blood from his face, Decker nods to the four deputies holding machine guns.

Responding, they mount the fire trucks and fire repeated short bursts at the flashes of gunfire coming from the mob. Decker motions for a megaphone. "Cease fire—hold your fire." Intermittent moans from the mobs wounded can be heard.

Decker warns the mob, "Snipers are in place. We have grenades and more machine guns. If anyone makes a hostile move, the deputies are instructed to shoot to kill—I mean business—now, take care of your wounded, and go home." The mob murmurs, then moves back. A wounded man is pleading as the mob disburses. "Help me, Jimmy—I'm hit. Where are you, Jimmy? I can't see! Someone—please—get me a doctor."

Meanwhile on Elm Street just past the Majestic Theater, as the crowd disperses, Benny and Tom Mott follow Shelby Morton as he walks with friends to a parking lot behind to the

Majestic Theater. They move in as Shelby Morton goes to his car. Unaware, his friends walk on. Quickly coming up behind him, Benny slips a rope over Shelby's head and jerks it tight, and then Mott puts a pillowcase over Shelby's head. Shelby's hands go to his throat. Tom Mott growls, "Where are the keys to your car, Morton?"Shelby Morton fumbles in his pocket and produces the car keys. Benny pushes Shelby Morton into the backseat as Mott slides under the wheel and drives the car from the parking lot, then turns onto Commerce Street, and continues across the Oak Cliff Viaduct. Inside the speeding car, Shelby Morton asks, "Where are you taking me—who are you?"

"You'll know me when you see me, Morton. We're taking you to a place you'll remember, and I guarantee you, you'll never forget." A light mist begins to fall and Tom Mott turns on the windshield wipers as the car continues into the night. After a time, the car lights pick up a road sign: Ferris, Texas, Population 118. A few moments later, the car turns left off of the main highway and follows a dark, bumpy, rutted wagon road.

After passing through a wooded area, the car stops in front of a gate. Tom Mott gets out and opens the gate. He gets back in and drives the car into a meadow surrounded by tall trees. A knurled old bois d'arc tree looms ahead, caught in the car's headlights. The tree's giant limbs form a Y, a little over three feet from the ground. After he stops the car, Tom Mott gets out and opens the back door; Benny hands the rope, which is still around Shelby's neck, to Tom Mott, who drags the prisoner to the front of the car and makes him kneel facing the headlights; he takes a cat-o'-nine-tails from a sack. Shelby Morton whimpers at the sound of the cat-o'-nine-tails swishing through the air.

Tom Mott jerks the pillowcase from Shelby Morton's head and the car lights blind him. "You remember me now? I promise you'll never forget me after tonight. I'm not gonna put you through the same bullshit ceremony you and the Klan put me through—I'm gonna get right to your whipping."

Tom Mott drags Shelby Morton to the torture tree and ties him securely, then rips Morton's shirt from his back. "Now, you cowardly son of a bitch—I'm gonna give you the same whipping you gave me, nothing more, nothing less—just be damn glad I don't kill you."The cat-o'-nine-tails swishes through the air striking Shelby Morton's back. He flinches and screams as nine whelps on his back ooze blood.

When the punishment is completed, Tom Mott and Benny drag a trembling, sobbing Shelby Morton to the car and shove him into the backseat.

The car returns to Dallas, and as they pass a Munger Avenue street sign, they slow then stop at 4126 Munger Avenue. The home is a two-story frame Plains-style house with a large front porch.

Benny wipes moisture from the car window. "This is it. This is the home of Hiram Westley—Grand Cyclops of the Invisible Empire."

They pull the trembling Klansman from the backseat, gag him, and place the pillowcase back over his head. They tie his hands and feet, carry him up the steps, and leave him trussed up on the porch at the front door. Benny rings the doorbell and they leave as Shelby Morton sobs and moans. Returning to the parked car, they watch as first the house lights come on, then the porch lights, revealing the name Hiram Westley on the mailbox. A bearded man, wearing a bathrobe, the Grand Cyclops of the Invisible Empire, Hiram Westley opens the door and discovers a man trembling, tied hand and foot lying on his porch. He kneels and removes the pillowcase from the victim's head and recognizes Shelby Morton, a fellow Klansman. The next morning, Bill Decker reads aloud from the list handed to him by Fred Lane, reporter for the *Dallas Times Herald*.

1. Jimmy Pullman, age 30, of 1306 North Pearl Street, shot in the right leg below the knee.
2. C. W. Wilson, age 23, of 3106 Cole Avenue, bullets in his right side and arm.
3. Dwight Stewart, age 18, of 822 South Cumberland Ave. Oak Cliff, shot in the abdomen, he is in critical condition.
4. Norval E. Duncan, age 20, of 2126 Leonard Street, shot in the left leg, lies in Parkland Hospital, the bone severed.
5. J. J. Younger, age 27, of 241 N. Boil Street, shot through the left forearm.
6. J. L. Swain, age 40, of 2018 Ross, back injured and his leg broken when he was knocked down and trampled by the crowd in their effort to escape the stream of water from the fire hoses.

"Fred, how bad is Stewart?"

Frowning, Fred replied, "I don't think he's gonna make it. Witness said he had just walked up when the shooting started. We found out that he works for the El Merito Pharmacy."

That same morning, a phone was ringing in an office with the name HIRAM WESTLEY, DENTIST, painted on the plate glass window of the door. The dentist enters the room and answers the phone.

"Dentist's office, Dr. Westley speaking."

Benny Binion, sitting at his desk, takes a cigar from his mouth.

"This is a message for the Grand Cyclops of the Invisible Empire. If any Dallas gambler or bootlegger comes under the Klan's whip again, the Grand Cyclops himself will be lynched while his family is made to watch."

Hiram Westley, visibly shaken, hangs up the phone, leaves his office, and puts a closed sign on the door.That afternoon at 4126 Munger Avenue, the home of the Grand Cyclops, moving men are placing furniture in a moving van as the dentist Hiram Westley and his family are moving to El Dorado, Arkansas, and Benny Binion has made a historical benchmark in Dallas history.

WARREN DIAMOND, CZAR OF DALLAS GAMBLING IN THE GAY '90S AND ROARING TWENTIES

THE 1911 WORLEY's City directory lists the name Warren H. Diamond, 1608 Cochran. Will Wilson's father, who was vice president of Cullum & Boren Sporting Goods in downtown Dallas, referred to Diamond as a product of the old North Dallas High School and the Papacita of gambling in Dallas.

> 09/09/03 Gordon Yoder, Warren Diamond's stepgrandson, 4331 Laren, Dallas, Texas 75244. North Dallas Rotary Club Brookhaven Country Club.

Elmer Grant Yoder and his wife, Nelly, Warren Diamond's cousin, had two children, a son, Wayne, and a daughter, Vivian.

Warren had been put in the Dallas jail as a result of a raid on his casino on the ground floor of the St. George Hotel on

Commerce Street, downtown Dallas. A childhood romance was rekindled when Nelly went to visit him in jail. Warren Diamond had only months before divorcing Zodie, his wife of eleven years. Diamond helped Nelly obtain a divorce from her husband and they were married. As a result of this matrimonial misconduct, the Catholic Church ostracized Warren Diamond.

Diamond's mother died and her body was interred in Calvary Catholic Cemetery on Hall Street next to Warren's father. Stricken with grief, Warren chose a beautiful wooded section of Grove Hill Cemetery and constructed a magnificent marble mausoleum at the cost of sixty thousand dollars.

Warren approached the church for permission to move his parents to the mausoleum, but was advised that it was against church doctrine and could not be permitted.

Not being one to let the church influence his thinking, Warren hired a team of qualified gravediggers and accompanied them to his parents' grave while they were removed under the cover of darkness.

Warren, his wife, Nelly, his parents, and Warren's older brother William all rest today in the marble mausoleum at Grove Hill Cemetery just off Samuels Boulevard in Dallas.

Gordon, the grandson, remembers moving to the Diamond mansion on Armstrong Parkway in Highland Park. A three-car garage housed a new Duesenberg that cost $15,000, a Lincoln chauffeur-driven touring car, and a Lincoln town car. It was the Duesenberg that Benny Binion drove for Warren Diamond.

Later when Wayne Yoder, Warren's stepson, got married, Warren built him a fine home in Highland Park. When the stepdaughter, Vivian, married, he built her and her husband a two-story stucco home in Mercedes, Texas.

Gordon continued to reminisce and recalled that Warren always came home in the afternoons. He carried a pistol in his pocket, which he always left on the hallway table. Gordon said no one ever said anything to him about the pistol, but he knew that he was not supposed to touch it and he never did.

After Warren's death, Nelly invested heavily in a Dallas cement company that went broke. It was only a few years later Nelly died as a result of an accident. She was warming herself by a gas heater and her flannel robe caught fire and she died from the burns.

THE ST. GEORGE HOTEL, THE MOST NEFARIOUS CASINO WEST OF NEW ORLEANS

WARREN DIAMOND INVESTED his winning in low-rent properties and became a Dallas slum lord. He took the income from his rental properties to what he developed into the most nefarious casino west of New Orleans, the St. George Hotel. Here Warren Diamond had his no-limit gambling that made Dallas and the St. George famous. If a cotton planter wanted to wager his fall harvest on a cut of the cards or one roll of the dice, Warren had instructed his dealers to take the wager and not bother to count the money. If the casino lost, then they would count to make the payment. If they won, they would count the money at their convenience.

Benny recalled his first visit to the St. George with Warren Diamond. They entered the lobby and the hotel clerk behind the registration desk looked up and greeted Mr. Diamond. As they walked through the lobby past the hotel café, Diamond said, "I'm going to show you the action." They walked into a hallway with a card room on each side before entering the casino. Overhead lights swung below three catwalks that traversed above the large casino. Hotel rooms opened onto an overhead balcony. Two men with shotguns peered down from above. Pointing out the men, Diamond said, "It is their job to watch and guard the action in the casino." There was a constant din of noise from two crap tables, and the whir and rattle of a roulette wheel sounded a reoccurring rhythm. A shout of excitement and profanity came from the patrons at one of the crap tables. Diamond led Benny into his office at the rear of the casino with a back door that opened into the alley.

> Steve Zareff, 205 Rosemont, Oak Cliff, whose father was a close friend of Sheriff Smoot Schmid, kept bar in the St. George Hotel. He provided the description of the hotel and casino, which was located across the street from the Adolphus Hotel, before the Baker Hotel was built, and is now One Main Place.

Benny was drawn to this action and started as a dice dealer for Diamond and later was made casino manager. Warren Diamond and Benny became fast friends. Christmas Day, Benny drove as he and Warren Diamond made the rounds of Diamond's rent houses. Diamond would have Benny stop and honk the horn at his tenant properties where children lived. When the children came running out, Warren Diamond would give them money.

Warren Diamond sat in a carved Spanish chair resembling a throne elevated against one wall. Large mirrors, encased in gold frames, hung on the wall opposite the throne-like chair. The room was always crowded with gamblers. Beautifully dressed women kibitz and would serve drinks for the gamblers.

It was in the month of November 1927 that a loud knock

on the casino's exterior door summons a muscular bouncer built like a pro football linebacker, who slid back a panel in the door and peered through. He opened the door and said, "Good evening, Mr. McLanhan. Good luck at the tables!"The bouncer steps aside to allow Dub McLanhan, a heavily built, well-dressed man who walked with a limp, to enter. He is accompanied by two tough-looking bodyguards. The pit boss, an older man with a serious demeanor, nods to McLanhan who ignores the pit boss and hands his hat and overcoat to the girl in the hat checkroom.The pit boss whispers to Benny, "That's Dub McLanhan, he just won sixty-three bales of cotton from Fred Merrill, a cotton plantation owner at the Greenville, Texas, gin. He has probably sold the cotton and will lay it all on the line and try to wipe Diamond out."

Dub McLanhan taps a white envelope impatiently against his hand.

Benny asks the pit boss, "Why does he act so pissed?"

"Last time McLanhan was here, Diamond took him for forty thousand. Diamond didn't even ask him how much money was in the envelope."

Dub McLanhan approaches Benny's crap table with the white envelope, obviously full of money. The players at the table make room for him. A hush falls over the casino as McLanhan slaps the envelope down on the table.

"Damn you, Diamond—I'll make you look this time!"

Not moving from his chair, Warren Diamond simply nods to the pit boss who asks the gambler whose turn it is to come out holding the dice, "Sir, would you mind if Mr. McLanhan shoots next ahead of you?"

The gambler looks at Dub McLanhan, answering, "I would consider it an honor to stand aside for you, Mr. McLanhan."

Dub McLanhan stiffly nods his thanks to the shooter.

Using the croupier's stick, Benny shoves a pair of dice to Dub McLanhan. "Good luck, sir. The odds will be in your favor coming out. A seven or an eleven will be a winner on the line."

Dub McLanhan places the white envelope on the line.

All the players get a bet down on the line with him. A hush falls over the room. Dub McLanhan picks up the dice, rolling them between his hands. He holds them to his mouth, whispering to the dice. He raises his right hand, rattling the dice, then throws them the length of the table and shouts, "Be there, sweet seven!" The dice bounce from the end of the table, a deuce and a three showing.

Benny chants, "Five—the shooter's point is five—a field winner—mark the number five."

Benny uses the croupier's stick to push the dice back to Dub McLanhan who again rolls the dice between his hands, holds them to his mouth, whispers, and again throws the dice.

Dub McLanhan shouts, "Give me a five right back!"

When the dice stop spinning, a deuce and an ace show. Benny holds the dice with the croupier's stick so they can be examined and chants, "Three, craps—all good shooters shoot craps—a winner on the field. The shooter's point is five—five will be a winner on the line."

Benny pushes the dice back to Dub McLanhan. Scowling, Dub picks up the dice and repeats his ritual and shouts, "Give me a five now, dice!"

The dice bounce from the end of the table, showing a three and a four.

Benny places his stick around the dice and holds them for all to see and chants, "Seven, a loser—it's all away—front line skinner, back line winner—a loser on the field."A simultaneous moan and gasp comes from the crowd as Benny holds the dice with the croupier's stick. "Better luck next time, Mr. McLanhan."

Ignoring Benny, Dub McLanhan, red-faced, wheels around to glare at Warren Diamond sitting in his great chair.

"Damn your soul to hell, Diamond—you may have won again, but I'll be back and break your ass yet!"Dub McLanhan bolts from the room, followed by his two bodyguards. The crowd's attention is on the pit boss as he counts the money from the envelope. He turns from the table holding up a fistful of money and shouts, "One hundred and seventy thousand dollars."

The gamblers and spectators break into a cheer and everyone talks excitedly. A well-dressed gambler in the crowd turns to a gentleman beside him. "We have just witnessed history; no doubt the largest wager on one roll of the dice in Texas—perhaps the world.

Benny recalled that Diamond used some of that money to buy a Duesenberg automobile. Only four hundred were manufactured that year. The car was German-built and the fastest car in the world at the time guaranteed to do 120 miles per hour on a flat track.

($10 in 1923 had the purchasing power of $350 in today's currency.)

GALVESTON MOB TRIES
TO TAKE OVER DALLAS

S AM MACEIO, THE Mafia don in Galveston, decided to take over the lucrative Dallas operation and a beer war broke out. The Dallas boys were getting the worst of it. Benny learned where a New Year's Eve party on December 31, 1929, was being held by the Galveston mob at the Tip Top Club, 2146 Commerce Street, close to Fair Park. Benny showed up a pump shotgun concealed under his overcoat and his fedora pulled low. He took out four of the Galveston mob's top players. The newspapers called it the Dallas County massacre and noted it was only nine months since the St. Valentine's Day massacre in Chicago. Sam Maceio soon called for a truce.

In 1930, Warren Diamond called a meeting of the Dallas Mafia and syndicate bosses. The meeting was held at the Mt. Vesuvius Restaurant run by Joe and Sam Campisi. When Diamond showed up, he had Murray Hughes, his attorney with him.

Diamond said, "The reason I have brought my attorney with

me tonight is I have been diagnosed with terminal cancer and I want no one to misunderstand what I am about to say. My wife and I have no children." Warren Diamond gestured to Benny Binion sitting next to him at his table and said, "But I see in Benny Binion everything I would like to have seen in a son of my own, so I am leaving the casino, all my political connections, my employees, and my business to Benny!" All the men stood and gave Diamond and Binion a standing ovation.

Benny Binion at the age of twenty-eight was catapulted to the number one man on the streets of Dallas. He was kingpin of Dallas bootlegging and the head of the powerful and very profitable Dallas gambling syndicate.

WARREN DIAMOND DEAD IN A POOL OF BLOOD, AN AUTOMATIC PISTOL AT HIS SIDE

IN APRIL 1932, Dallas Homicide Captain Will Fritz's office door burst open and a dispatcher handed him a memo. His eyes narrowed as he read the report. Warren C. Diamond had been found in the bathroom of his Highland Park mansion in a pool of blood, an automatic pistol at his side.

Captain Fritz pulled up at Diamond's mansion at 4224 Armstrong Parkway. He found Diamond with a gaping hole in his right temple. George Foote, Diamond's bookkeeper, was present. Will Fritz drew Foote aside in the library.

Detective Fritz asked, "To your knowledge, was anyone crossways with Mr. Diamond?"

Foote answered, "Everyone except a few petty politicians loved him."

"Now, Mr. Foote, I want you to tell me everything you know about Mr. Diamond, his businesses, and his career. Leave no detail out."

George Foote began, "Mr. Diamond was born March 22, 1877, in New Orleans, Louisiana. His parents and an older brother were just off the ship from Ireland, fleeing the potato famine. The family later moved to Dallas, and Warren grew up a tough, churchgoing, and street-fighting Irishman fluent in Cajun French. He was sometimes referred to as Knuckles Diamond, because in his youth, he settled many disputes with a swat of the hand, wearing brass knuckles."

Fritz asked, "How did he get involved in gambling?"

Foote continued, "What I heard was that Diamond began to gamble impulsively as a child in New Orleans. He had a quick mind that could handle numbers like a modern-day computer. He astounded strangers at the Dallas freight yard superintendent's office by adding the numbers on boxcars as the slow-moving freight trains pulled out. He would spit out the total sum as if it were hot saltwater. Then Diamond would offer to bet that his figures were right. If he was challenged, the yard superintendent would run a tally from the freight manifest, which always verified Diamond's total.

"As a kid in high school, Diamond gambled his way into a Dallas fortune. Whether he was shooting craps in an Oak Cliff alley, or drawing three cards at poker in a hotel card parlor, he was ruthless and his composure betrayed no emotion. He always won. By the time he was twenty-one, he was half-owner of the most notorious gambling den in Dallas, the St. George Hotel. In 1911, Diamond, at the of age thirty-four, purchased a prestigious Dallas home at 1608 Cochran, across the street from Urseline Academy, just inside the neighborhood called Munger Place. On the outskirts of Dallas at that time, it was just a short carriage ride downtown to the St. George Hotel.

"Diamond became a millionaire gambler and could fix anything. His henchmen did his work for him and no one talked. One of his favorite ploys was fixing the baseball games between Dallas and Ft. Worth. He paid a twenty-five-dollar bonus to any Dallas player who would punch out a Ft. Worth player."

Captain Fritz laughed and said, "Sure, I remember those fights."

Foote went on with the story. "Diamond bet heavily on just about anything, fixing the odds and the outcome when possible, yet this big Irishman had a host of very loyal friends."

"Now, how does Ben Whitaker fit in with Diamond?"

Foote replied, "As his war chest grew and with a plan in place, Diamond sat at the back door of the Dallas banks buying delinquent real estate notes. Ben Whitaker's father had been a dealer for Diamond at the St. George Hotel. Young Whitaker was a bright, streetwise lieutenant of Diamond's. He guided Diamond in the purchase of hotels, nightclubs, gambling casinos, and brothels. Whitaker was Diamond's strong right arm and deal man, young enough to be his son. He was courageous, likable, well-educated, and polished."

George Foote smiled and recalled, "With the enactment of the Volstead Act, prohibition came to Dallas. Diamond's moneymaking machine went into fast-forward. There is a story that late one afternoon in 1923, Diamond noticed a kid selling whiskey from the back of a wagon at the hitching rail of the St. George Hotel. Diamond said nothing, but went into the hotel and told Whitaker, 'A big good-looking Irish kid is selling booze off of the back of a wagon in front of our hotel.' Diamond instructed Whitaker to call a policeman that they had on their payroll to arrest the kid. When confronted by the police officer, the kid handled himself well. He circled the cop to get the afternoon sun to his back and into the policeman's eyes. Then he struck the officer and took his pistol away from him. As the officer sat on the ground, he said to the kid, 'Damn, son, you got a mean streak in you. What are you gonna do now?'

"The kid told the policeman, 'I'm gonna take the bullets out of your pistol and give it back to you.' Diamond told the young Irishman. 'Kid, I was watching you. You handle yourself pretty well.' The kid said, 'You're Mr. Diamond, aren't you?' Diamond answered, 'Yes, I am,' and shook the kid's hand. 'I'm Benny Binion, Mr. Diamond, and I want us to be friends.'

"Instead of admonishing Benny for selling booze without permission, he invited Benny inside the St. George Hotel for coffee. Benny explained that he was selling Joe Civello's booze from a warehouse on Pocahontas Street. 'Civello cumulates beer from all the local bootleggers at five dollars a barrel.' Diamond in turn explained that he owned not only the St. George, but controlled several restaurants, speakeasies, and brothels. 'Benny, you're a good Irish boy. Go back and tell Civello I want to set a meeting. It's time we get things organized.'

"The meeting was set and Dallas was organized. Benny Binion was the enforcer and salesman for the newly formed cartel. Nearly everyone went along. Benny was a good salesman. He had to call on some businesses twice. When Benny had to make a second visit, he took two guerrillas with him, one with a can of gasoline. If the proprietor refused the second time, Benny would hold a shotgun on the proprietor and the gorilla with the gasoline can began pouring, the other gorilla would light a match and look at Benny.

"It wasn't long before Benny had all the business in Dallas sewed up. Those new bootleggers who didn't check in with Benny before starting their business usually had a run of bad luck. Either the police force, supplied with inside information from Whitaker, put the competitor away or Binion did. Whitaker was six years older than Benny and had senior rank in Diamond's organization. Benny developed into Diamond's strong right-arm man, responsible for enforcing the rough stuff on the streets. He was able to buy beer at $5 a barrel from the independent producers that he had organized, and Diamond had a ready market at $45 a barrel.

"Dallas consumed a million and a half barrels a year. I'll leave the arithmetic to you. There was plenty of money for everyone. Diamond's money was rolling in so fast that he couldn't find enough ways to spend it. So in addition to buying all the rent property he could get his hands on, he loaned vast sums of money to judges, politicians, police captains, and court officials.

"Diamond's interest rates were high, but in some cases, Whitaker did not push elite customers for payment, rather he arranged settlements in other ways. A payment in kind, you might say, perhaps the quashing of an indictment, or misplaced evidence pertaining to one of Diamond's rumrunners, strong-arm boys, or prostitutes. As the twenties roared, so did Diamond. He used Ben Whitaker to handle the politicians and Binion took care of the streets." Foote concluded, "That's all I know."

Captain Fritz nodded and commented, "Well, that sums it up then, money wasn't a problem and he had no enemies."

Captain Fritz returned to the bathroom where the body lay, a .38 Colt automatic pistol beside the body. He took a pencil and ran it down the barrel of the weapon. Fritz found a paper sack and placed the weapon inside and left for the station. Fingerprints and ballistics all matched and Justice of the Peace Ben H. Fly pronounced death due to self-inflicted gunshot wound.

BENNY BINION, THE BROKEN BUMPER WARRIOR

BENNY WORKED IN the casino some nights into the wee hours of the morning. One of those late nights, when Benny left work and got into his Buick automobile, he noticed four cars pulling in behind him. He suspected, just as Hiram Westley had feared, that the Klan had marked Benny for threatening the Klan Grand Cyclopes and trouble was going to begin again.

Benny's Buick was about to enter the Commerce Street Bridge when a truck from out of nowhere with its lights turned off rammed into the side of the Buick, upending it. One side of the car doors jammed from the collision and the others blocked lying on the ground; Benny was trapped.

He kicked out the windshield and emerged over the hood of the car. His hand closed on a loose piece of the broken front bumper lying in the street as a group of Klansmen's cars encircled him, their headlights blinding him.

A voice from the glaring circle of lights called to Benny. "Will you surrender to us?"

Benny responded, "Not unless you are a friend of Bobby Lee!" an answer that would only make sense to a native of Pilot Grove or Binion family.

Another voice from the glaring circle of lights shouted, "There is nothing like whipping a smart-ass gambler!" As if this were a signal, the mob advanced. Benny stood his ground, keeping the overturned Buick to his back. Like a Viking warrior with a battle-ax, he swung the twisted bumper smashing and hacking, drawing blood from Klansmen with every blow.

Benny hoped for help from the Dallas police. But it was Deputy Sheriff Bill Decker who stepped from a sheriff's car and fired three shots into the night air. Like a referee's whistle in a football game, all activity stopped. Those of the Klan who could still stand were administering to the moaning, bleeding wounded, stacked around Benny.

By the time the Dallas police arrived, Deputy Sheriff Bill Decker had Benny cuffed and in the backseat of his squad car. The Dallas police called for ambulances and nineteen Klan members were taken to Parkland Hospital. Later at the county jail, Decker saw to it that Benny was taken to the infirmary. Decker explained that just to be on the safe side, he would make Benny a trustee, giving him the run of the jail. The men agreed that it would be a good idea to get things sorted out before letting Benny back out on the street.

The next day, Benny went before Judge Kenneth Miller, who had a reputation as a judge in favor of fair play. When asked, Benny chose not to prefer charges against the Klan members. Judge Miller remarked that he felt the Klansmen had learned their lesson that six of the nineteen men taken to Parkland Hospital had not been released.

The *Dallas Times Herald* headlines read, BENNY BINION THE BUMPER WARRIOR SENDS NINETEEN TO PARKLAND HOSPITAL.

Joe Ianni's restaurant Vesuvius held a party honoring

Benny. He was the man of the hour. He had delivered an ultimatum to the Grand Cyclops of the Invisible Empire and added insult to injury to the Klan's dignity by sending nineteen of them to the hospital.

Hughes Monroe, a guest, was introduced to the group; he was a brilliant Dallas attorney and was well-known for his devotion to fair play. His brief speech praising Benny further endeared him to the group.

Joe Civello spoke on the subject of ferocity. He praised Benny because he defended himself with ferocity at the right time and at the right place. Civello spoke of ferocity as a precious weapon that must always have an important purpose and be used intelligently. He ended his remarks and gave Benny the floor to reiterate his encounter with the Klan.

Benny stayed late in the smoke-filled room in order to speak with Civello about a mission he wanted to undertake. There were a number of gangs in Dallas that were all making money in spite of their disorganization.

Benny envisioned a cartel that would identify and harness the talents and energies of each gang and its members. Those small gangs that would not come into the cartel would simply be eliminated.

Benny explained, "I'm an honest gambler, house odds take care of me." He pointed out that casino dice games under the cartel's control would be a straight game, allowing the operators their profits. The end results: anyone could run a game as long as they had a bank roll and could pay the syndicate twenty-five percent of the profit off the top.

In return, the syndicate would supply police protection and a roster of friendly politicians. This worked in a wondrous manner, and Benny, when interviewed, stated that he was paying the mayor of Dallas sixty thousand dollars a year and each councilman twenty thousand and business was good.

BIRTH OF A BUSINESS

JOHN CANAVAN WAS the sales manager for the American Standard Life Insurance Company in Dallas. His granddaughter who was a nurse for St. Paul Hospital told the following story.

It was almost lunchtime on a hot July afternoon in 1925. Grandfather and a new recruit were cold canvassing on Forest Avenue close to the old State Theater. They went up a flight of stairs to a second-story office over a grocery store and knocked on the door. A voice from within said, "Come in."

Entering the office, a friendly man behind a desk said, "Come in, have a seat." The two salesmen made themselves comfortable. Grandfather had assumed that Mr. Binion was in the grocery business since his office was above the store.

It wasn't long and Grandfather had launched into a sales presentation proposing life insurance for Mr. Binion. He explained cash values premium collections and, of course, death benefits.

Mr. Binion listened carefully asking an occasional question. When Grandfather took out an application and began filling it out, Mr. Binion asked Grandfather to come back the next day at the same time alone.

Grandfather returned the next day alone as requested. Mr. Binion again greeted his knock on the door with "Come in." Entering the office, John was introduced to a second man whose name was Willie Friedon.

"John," Benny said, looking at the card that had been left with him the day before, "Mr. Friedon is my partner and we have been discussing starting our own insurance company and would like to have you listen to our ideas." Benny motioned for John to sit down.

Willie continued, "We have taken the idea of insurance and turned around to make it a possibility of getting rich without having to die."

John looked puzzled and Willie continued. "You are a sales manager and you have a number of salesmen that collect insurance premiums weekly from families." Willie lit a cigar and Benny offered one to John.

Leaning back in his chair, John Canavan made himself comfortable as he lit his cigar, watching Willie Friedon through the smoke. He thought to himself, "This could be a lifetime opportunity to be in on the incubation of a new company."

Willie continued, "John, we want you to consider being the sales manager and comptroller of an insurance company that pays off to someone every week without anyone dying."

John interrupted, "Where would the money come from, and how much would the beneficiary be paid and why?"

Benny started laughing and said, "I told you he was smart." Willie stood up and started pacing. "John, the money would come from your salesmen collecting premiums from American Standard customers just like they do now, only they would be buying our policies too."

John was visibly shaken with the idea of using customers from his company to start a new one. "This didn't seem right," he was thinking.

Benny sensed this and interrupted John's thoughts. "It doesn't mean they would drop their American Standard policies, and you and your salesmen wouldn't have to quit their job."

Willie continued, "John, let's do some arithmetic, let's say that we got a thousand customers paying fifty cents a week and each customer that buys a policy gets a policy with a number on it. John, the company has collected five hundred dollars. Do you follow me, are my figures right?" John nodded in agreement. Willie continued, "The company has five hundred dollars and we hold a drawing. All the policy numbers of our customers will be put in a wire wheel. The number that is drawn from the wheel gets paid, let's say, $300, that would be a six hundred percent return on the fifty-cent premium and is equal to two months' wages or more for most of the customers."

John picked up on this real quick and said, "If we had more customers, the company's profit would be greater."

Benny laughed and hollered. "Eeeee! I told you he was a smart one, Willie."

With the first winner receiving the three hundred dollars, the news spread like wildfire. This at last was an opportunity for a working man to get a breath of fresh air, and with his wife's permission. There had been many arguments in the working families of Dallas when Dad explained why there was no paycheck due to cards or dice. The times were so hard that five or six dollars a week was just not enough money to get by on, and in desperation, everyone turned to gambling.

Business was so good because other insurance men representing other companies came to the Binion's policy business. In a short time, the drawings were held once daily. As one part of Dallas got organized, other parts began to come in with premiums. The logical thing to do was to start another policy operation for that part of town.

Dallas was divvied into four sections, and the four policy

wheels were designated High Noon, the Mother Load, White and Green, and the Harlem Queen. The sales force was furnished with a dream book, which interpreted dreams and helped the players choose their numbers. One player for instance had dreamed of bananas. The dream book interpreted this dream as the number 777.

Sunday, April 29, 2001, Rock Creek-Bar-b-Q Club Grand Prairie, Texas, noon. Wild Life Road off of Beltline Road interview with George Boyce, forty-year employee of the *Dallas Times Herald*.

Dee Abahaus, a professional light heavyweight fighter that lived on Floyd Street near Baylor Hospital in Dallas, came to see Binion because his manager Bobby Cook had lost the purse from his latest fight in a crap game at the old Southland Hotel run by Binion's boys.

Storming into Binion's office that was located on Main Street in the back of a grocery store, Dee found Benny talking on the phone as he burst through his office door.

Angry at first, Dee was ready to turn over Binion's desk and get right in the middle of him. Binion, however, with the sparkle of a leprechaun in his blue eyes after listing to Dee's complaint, said, "Take it easy, Dee, I'll tell ya how you can get your money back in spades. I need a man that can handle his fists to run a collection route for me."

Dee seemed to cool down as he turned and took a chair in Binion's office. "I don't want to do anything crooked," he said, meeting Benny's intense stare.

"First of all, I want us to be friends," Binion began, "this is the way it works, I have an insurance business that I run. We have salesmen that collect premiums from the policy buyers, and at the end of each day, we draw three numbers at random and the name and address on the policy with those numbers is declared the beneficiary of the insurance bank. That policy holder wins 600 percent of whatever size premium he has paid."

Benny continued, "If the policy holder has paid a twenty-five-cent premium, he wins $150, if he has paid fifty cents, he wins $300."

Benny's eyes narrowed. "Our problem is times are tough and our salesmen are always in danger of being held up and robbed." Benny intentionally stopped talking and studied Dee's reaction.

Dee nodded and said, "I don't see anything crooked about that, but how do I fit into all this?"

Benny responded, "What I need is a man like yourself that can protect my salesmen and collect the day's premiums from them and deliver to my bank to be counted." Benny paused again, studying Dee's face.

Dee asked, "Suppose one of these hoodlums has a gun or a knife?" Benny got up from his desk and looked out the window as he spoke. "Dee, it probably won't come to that, but if I were you, I would carry a weapon that would resolve any unforeseen problems."

Dee asked, "What does the job pay, Mr. Binion?"

Turning back to face Dee, Benny replied, "Dee, it will be a lot more than you ever made fighting. You will get five percent of all the money you bring in. We have four insurance companies and they all run about eight hundred to a thousand dollars a day. You will be the premium collection manager for one of the companies."

Benny watched Dee closely and he saw the wheels in Dee's mind counting out his daily five percent.

Standing and looking squarely at Binion, Dee asked, "What about my fight purse that Bobby lost to your crap game?"

Benny stared hard at Dee. "I want you to understand that the game is honest, it's important that you know that. How much was the purse, Dee?"

"My part was forty dollars, Mr. Binion."

Not pausing or answering, Benny reached in his pocket and pealed two twenty-dollar bills from a large roll of money and handed it to Dee. "Like I said, Dee, I want us to be friends regardless of what you decide about the job."

Dee took the money and said, "Thank you, Mr. Binion." Benny walked from behind his desk and put his arm on Dee's shoulders as he walked him to the door. Dee paused at the door and said, "Mr. Binion, I want that job, when can I start my new job?"

In addition to his new job as collections manager for Binion's insurance company, Dee got a job with the *Dallas Times Herald* as route manager, and it was only a matter time till the web of Binion's policy premium collections was extended to include the newsboys working Dee's route.

According to Mr. Boyce, many of the people with the *Dallas Times Herald* were working for Mr. Binion at that time.

AUGUST 26, 1990
A DALLAS DOCTOR WRITES HIS
MEMORIES OF BENNY BINION

How I remember Benny Binion
Emerson Emory, MD

SHORTLY AFTER CHRISTMAS Day 1989, the Associated Press and the New York Times News Service wired a story of the death of Benny Binion of Las Vegas. Picked up by local dailies, the article centered primarily upon Mr. Binion's encounter with the law in Dallas over fifty years ago. Perhaps present-day black citizens of this city paid little attention to the account, but a few remain who recall the good during Mr. Binion's stay in Dallas.

The 1929 crash, although seldom considered to have an effect on the black families, caused the loss of jobs, which black men held as janitors in local corporations. Black women were forced to bear the support of their families by employment as domestics in the park cities. This condition remained until the Japanese attack on Pearl Harbor in 1941 and the increased spending by the government which followed.

It was during this in-between period of time that Mr. Binion introduced the game of "policy" to the black community. Although described by the local media as a fifty-cent quarter rigged game, policy would actually allow the player to play for a nickel or dime. Ten cents would get the winner ten dollars. Even better, the game provided employment for many black men who had no other means of gaining financial aid. A con game policy? Not any more than the present-day state-run lottery.

The media seems to take great joy in pointing to the illegal nature of policy, but as one who reaps some of the benefits, I shall always remember Benny Binion for other reasons which accompanied the game of lottery wheel policy.

I remember Benny as a person who gave my unemployed father a job so that my mother and I could eat. I remember the pride that my father showed whenever he collected his small earnings, the results of miles of walking in the community.

I remember the expression of joy on my mother's face after learning that ten cents of her hard-earned money had netted the sum of ten dollars when she won. Yes, there was a look of despair when she lost, yet play again she did as soon as possible. You see, the thought of winning ten dollars was far more beneficial than the actual sum that she earned in the kitchens of University and Highland Park working from sunup to dark six days a week and sometimes seven days a week.

I remember the opportunity given to me as a preteenager to earn money by delivering "policy slips" to customers. Illegal, maybe, but no more than the present-day football pots.

I remember trucks, laden with apples and oranges, which Mr. Binion had parked next to the policy shack behind the old State Theater during the Christmas season. Sometimes the only gift the neighborhood kids would receive from Santa.

I remember the pleasure shown by Mr. Binion when several

of the Washington/Lincoln Alumni Association of Dallas (meeting in Las Vegas several years ago) after presenting a plaque presented to Benny, accepted by his son Jack, journeyed to his home to present the plaque in person. We spent the best part of the evening talking about the days in Dallas and of the men who had known Benny and admired him.

As far as I am concerned, Benny Binion did no wrong. Until our society becomes aware of the fact that brushes with the law do not always destroy the compassion of all men who are unfortunate enough to encounter its wrath, then we will continue to be reminded of acts under the guise of justice and forget those deeds for the sake of humanity. As it was said of Caesar:

The evil that men do lives after them,
The good is oft entered with their bones.

If my parents were alive today, I'm sure they would join me in saying, "Thanks to you, Benny, for having been a part of our lives. Thank you for giving us hope when all was despair and for bringing happiness when all had been lost. May you forever rest in peace, knowing that there are still those that remember."

(Dr. Emory is a native Dallasite, a practicing physician with offices in South Dallas and founding president of the Washington/Lincoln Alumni Association of Dallas, Inc.)

LUNCH AT THE BLUE FRONT CAFÉ

HAL ALEXANDER HOOD was sworn into office as sheriff of Dallas County, January 1, 1929. During his tenure as deputy sheriff under Sheriff Dan Hartson, he was appointed chief deputy in charge of raids on bootlegging and illegal stills. The main plank in Hood's political platform for sheriff had been to completely rid Dallas County of the illegal alcohol trade. He was backed by the prohibitionist party and the Women's Christian Temperance Union, which resulted in not only Hood's election but also a clean sweep of the old guard in the Dallas city hall.

Like a blue Texas Norther, the new sheriff's attacks on the manufacture and sales of illegal alcohol swept across Dallas County. Hood was confiscating an impressive amount of illegal alcohol.

To celebrate his election, a public rally was held on Main Street downtown Dallas. The sheriffs' deputies were smashing cases of liquor with axes as the Women's Temperance cheered.

Some of Benny's trucks loaded with shine were involved in the demonstration.

Benny had just finished lunch inside the Blue Front Café when the new sheriff's celebration and the Women's Christian Temperance Union brouhaha started just outside on Main Street. He was talking with Willie, the proprietor's son. Willie's thirteen sisters waited tables for the customers of the fine German restaurant. The family mother who ran the cash register was always referred to as "the Boss Mama."

Willie was in charge of the preparation of the mouthwatering prime rib that was always ready at eleven o'clock each morning. Polish sausage, sauerkraut, German potato salad, navy beans, rye bread, horse radish, and draught beer, which always brought in a noonday stampede. It was the custom for patrons to share their table with complete strangers, a common practice to accommodate the noonday rush. The Blue Front Café was the very essence of the Spirit of Dallas at that time in our history.

The customer's meal was often interrupted by a knockdown, drag-out, cuss fight between the sisters as they waited on tables. The patrons would stop eating and watch in amusement until one of the girls would leave in a huff. The profane arguments were colorful and added to the café's reputation; the patrons would always clap and cheer at the conclusion of each confrontation.

While Benny was standing at the front window next to the cash register, he heard the commotion in the street. He looked out to see one of his trucks being attacked by the Dallas County deputies with axes in hand as newspaper reporters took pictures of the action. It was a sickening sight to see all that good whiskey running down the gutter toward the lower end of Main Street.

Benny left by the back door of the café and came out in the alley about a half a block below the activity. He noticed that two Dallas police cars were parked on the same side of the street as his trucks. He knew his trucks were a lost cause and watched the chaotic action in the street. Benny's reaction was quick. He took a book of matches from his pocket, ignited them, and stepped to the curb and dropped the flaming packet into the river of whiskey flowing down the street and into the storm sewer. A subtle blue flame raced in two directions, one toward the sewer, the other under the two police cars and Benny's trucks.

All pandemonium broke loose as the deputies and the Women's Christian Temperance Union ladies scrambled to get away from the river of flames. There was a big whoosh as the flames in the sewer belched back fire seeking more oxygen. The police cars and Benny's trucks were engulfed in flames and the gas tanks soon exploded as the crowd screamed and ran for cover.

Benny caught a cab and laughed all the way back to his office. The fire department came too late. The fire was completely out of control. The *Dallas Times Herald* reported that twenty-two automobiles were destroyed, buildings were damaged, but fortunately, no one was injured.

A DALLAS SHERIFF GETS CAUGHT WITH HIS HAND IN THE TILL

As told by Mr. Dow Fuller, 3117
Sharon Street, Dallas, Texas

MY BROTHER, JAMES W. Fuller, worked for the Dallas police force for fourteen years. He and his partner George Brook, a short, stout man called "Stubby," worked as detectives known as plainclothes men in those days. The two men knew they could depend on each other and were inseparable.

They answered a complaint of gambling at the Maurice Hotel. They found some big shots involved in a card game and arrested them. The next day, Chief J. W. Trammel called the detectives into his office and told them to stay away from the Maurice Hotel.

James was angry when they left the chief's office and told Stubby, "Now when I took this job, I took an oath to uphold the law, and if I'm called again about gambling at the Maurice Hotel, I'll do my job and arrest the gamblers again."

It was less than a week when the two detectives received another call from the management of the Maurice Hotel complaining of gambling and they arrested the gamblers and brought them to the station.

The following day, Chief Trammel called the partners into his office and told them to turn in their guns and their badges. They were being busted back to walking a beat. Mr. Fuller said his brother told the chief, "No, this will be my last day." And he threw his badge down on the chief's desk. "You can have your badge back, but I ain't gonna give you the pistol, I paid for that myself, and it belongs to me!"

Dallas County Sheriff Hal Hood had been after James to go to work for him as a deputy sheriff for some time. He took the job with the sheriff's department as a detective and was assigned a partner by the name of Bill Large.

Stubby stayed with the Dallas police department and, on occasion, rode with James and his partner Bill Large. On one of these occasions, the three men were working deep night patrol. In those days, the deputies used their own cars. Deputy Large was driving his car when they spotted a parked car on an abandoned road close to the Kaufman County line.

The sheriff's department was looking for two escaped convicts, and as they drove past the parked car, they saw two men inside the car asleep. Stubby wanted to question the two men, and James told Deputy Large to stop beside the parked car. James got out of the car, but before Stubby could get out, Deputy Large gunned his car and pulled away. Stubby jumped from the moving car to assist James; Large continued down the road and parked out of range of any gunfire.

It was summertime and the windows of the parked car were rolled down. James went to the driver's side window and shined his flashlight inside the car on the sleeping man. He saw a pistol on the front seat and a rifle in the backseat. Taking no chance, he pushed his pistol into the face of the sleeping man and told him, "If you move, I'll kill you." By this time, Stubby was on the other side of the car to assist and the two men surrendered.

The men they captured were the escaped convicts the sheriff's department was looking for. The next day, James went to Sheriff Hal Hood and told him that he wanted another partner. "Deputy Large was not dependable when things get hot." Sheriff Hood replied, "Bill Large is an influential man, related to a lot of Dallas people, and for that reason, I won't do anything until after the upcoming election."

A couple of weeks later on June 11, 1932, at about 2:00 a.m., Deputies James Fuller and Bill Large were given an assignment to check out a burglary complaint from a Mrs. Gus Williams who lived on a farm in the southern part of Dallas County on the Wheatland Desoto Road.

What the two lawmen did not know at the time was Mrs. Williams, along with Benny Binion, was running a bootlegging operation from her home. While they were questioning Mrs. Williams about the burglary complaint, "whiskey hijackers," who had earlier that night burglarized the home, were hiding and watching from a peach orchard close to the house.

The whiskey hijackers, as they were called in those days, were hated both by the lawmen and the bootleggers. Leroy Hardin, Audrey James, Roy Archer, and Bill James waited in the darkness thinking more whiskey was to be delivered to the Williams home that night.

The whiskey hijackers called from the darkness demanding entry. Warren Williams, the nephew of Mrs. Williams, was in the living room with Mrs. Williams and her newborn grandson. Deputy Fuller ordered Warren to put the baby under the bed and place pillows around him. Then he ordered Williams to slide a large cabinet across the back door.

From outside, a hijacker hollered at Mrs. Williams to light a lamp. Deputy Fuller told her not to, but she was frightened and lit the lamp anyway. The hijackers started shooting into the house. Two screen doors opened onto a broad front porch.

As the hijackers advanced onto the front porch, Deputy Fuller returned fire with a .44-caliber revolver. Leroy Hardin fell. James bullet had found its mark. But Hardin got up and started toward the other door. James shouted, "He's coming to your door, Bill—"

Crouched behind a sofa in the other room, Bill replied, "I got him!"

Hardin could see no one in the second room. He wheeled and fired again at Deputy Fuller, his shot hitting Fuller in the head. Panicked, the hijackers fled into the darkness.

Warren Williams, the nephew, jumped out the back window of the house and ran across the pasture to a neighbor's house and called for an ambulance for the wounded Deputy Fuller.

Mrs. Williams later testified at Hardin's murder trial that Deputy Bill Large went into a clothes closet and hid. He wasn't watching the front door at all and that's when Leroy Hardin fired the second time, his bullet hitting Deputy James Fuller in the head.

At the time of the shooting, Stubby, James's former Dallas police partner and friend, was walking his beat on Elm Street when he got word James had been shot. Someone in the police department phoned a call box on Stubby's beat and told him that James had been shot and was en route to Methodist Hospital.

Stubby went directly to the hospital and waited for the ambulance. James was still conscious and recognized Stubby. James told Stubby, "You should have been there with me, Stubby. It got real hot."

Stubby replied, "If I had been there, partner, they would have carried us both out together, or we would have both walked away." James then told Stubby through clenched teeth, "Tell Hall Hood, Bill won't stick!" Two days later on June 13, 1932, James died.

As a result of a phone call from Benny Binion, Leroy Hardin was captured by Captain Will Fritz, of Dallas Homicide. Hardin received a ninety-nine-year sentence for the murder of Deputy James Fuller.

Roy Archer was killed in Alma, Arkansas, while holding up a gas station and a grocery store. An Arkansas highway patrolman, who was a friend of the owners of the gas station, stopped in to visit and he caught Archer in the act of robbery. When Archer turned on the highway patrolman, gun in hand, the patrolman shot and killed him.

Mrs. Williams testified at Hardin's murder trial that she was paying Sheriff Hal Hood $40-a-month protection money for her bootlegging business that she ran from her home. The then-incumbent Sheriff Hood was defeated by his opponent Sheriff Smoot Schmid in the election later that fall. Folks said that her testimony in the murder trial cost Hal Hood the election.

KILLERS WITHOUT BADGES

In 1932, Ross Sterling was governor of Texas. His political opponent was Miriam "Ma" Ferguson. Her campaign slogan was "Two Governors for the Price of One." When her husband, Jim Ferguson, ran for governor, he recognized that ninety percent of the income in the state of Texas was agro income and he had nicknamed himself "Farmer Jim Ferguson."

Farmer Jim was later impeached because he put the state's money in his bank in Temple, Texas, and spent it. The Texas Rangers were called in, and their investigation brought about Governor Ferguson's impeachment.

In the 1932 election, all of the Texas Rangers campaigned against Ma Ferguson, but she was elected and was inaugurated January 13, 1933. That afternoon, she fired all forty-four Texas Rangers.

Manuel "Lone Wolfe" Gonzalles and Captain Frank Hamer, who could kill a man with no more emotion than most people feel when they step on a bug, found themselves unemployed in the depth of the Great Depression.

The two unemployed Texas Rangers, without their badges, conspired and came to Dallas in Gonzalles's bulletproof Chrysler sedan and checked into the Adolphus Hotel. Manuel Gonzalles called Benny Binion on the phone and told him, "Benny, this is Manuel Gonzalles, Frank Hamer and I are in room 633 at the Adolphus Hotel. Come over here now, we want to talk to you."

Benny said he was frightened. He knew that Manuel Gonzalles had killed 152 men and Frank Hamer had killed 110, but he did as he was told. He went to the Adolphus and got on the elevator and rode to the sixth floor and went to the door of room 633. Benny said, "When I knocked on the door, the character that came to the door would have been comical had he not been so dangerous." Manuel Gonzalles opened the door, he was barefooted and wearing only a bathrobe, but he had on a leather holster with two six-shooters strapped on over his bathrobe.

Gonzalles said, "Come in, kid." As Benny stepped past Gonzalles, he flipped up the collar on his bathrobe and said, "I been killing people for the state of Texas for the last twelve years and all I got to show for it is this worn-out old bathrobe."

Frank Hamer, a large man well over six feet tall weighing in excess of two hundred pounds, lumbered across the room and pushed Benny Binion into a chair and said, "Sit down, punk!"

Benny's hand started for a .38 Colt automatic in a shoulder holster under his coat, but while he was still making his move, he heard the simultaneous clicking of the hammers on Gonzalles's revolvers and he was staring into the muzzles of those deadly pistols.

Frank Hamer laughed and said, "Fast ain't he, punk?"

Holding his pistols only inches from Binion's face, Gonzalles said, "The reason we called you up here tonight is because we are going into business with you here in Dallas. We are going to be your new partners and it's going to be a ninety-ten split."

Benny, livid with rage, shouted, "Go ahead and shoot your goddamned pistols! I'm not giving anybody ninety percent of my business just because they point loaded guns at me!"

Gonzalles laughed, twirled his pistols, and put them back in their holsters. Frank Hamer laughed as Gonzalles, waving his empty hand, said, "No! No! Benny, you got it all wrong, you're keeping the long end, we're taking the short end of the business."

Benny saw the humor in his mistake and began laughing with the ex-rangers and the three men became fast friends. Lone Wolf Gonzalles worked for Benny Binion for the next four years. Until the politicians down in Austin were speculating on who they should choose to head up the newly formed Texas Department of Public Safety.

Someone suggested Manuel T. Gonzalles in Dallas, and he was appointed the head of the Texas Department of Public Safety.

Frank Hamer worked for Benny Binion for the next eleven years, but he did take a six weeks' leave of absence long enough to help the Dallas County sheriff's department track down and ambush Bonnie and Clyde Barrow on a back road in Gibsland, Louisiana.

End Note

1. Benny Binion's story of hiring two killers without their badges to help him control the streets of Dallas was one he loved and often told.

PRETTY BOY FLOYD

CHARLES ARTHUR FLOYD was born in rural Bartow County, Georgia, on February 3, 1904—one of seven children of a tenant farmer. When he was seven years old, the family moved to the town of Hanson, Oklahoma, where his father was employed as a sharecropper and, in between crops, learned the trade of manufacturing bootleg whiskey.

Young Floyd was fascinated with the stories told about Henry Starr, the Cherokee Bad Man, who was a legendary bank robber throughout Oklahoma and Kansas. When Floyd was nine, Starr robbed thirteen banks in a three-month period. His picture blazed on the front page of the local paper, and the kids would whisper about where he might strike next. When Floyd played with other children, he always insisted on being the Cherokee Kid.

He worked his father's dirt-poor farm, digging in the land that was soon to become the Great Dust Bowl. It was hard work, but the unschooled Floyd was never heard to complain.

After the day's work and on the weekends, he would find

release in hellin' around and drinking a local brew called Choctaw beer. It seemed that he constantly had a bottle of Choctaw in his hand and his friends began to call him "Chock."

In 1921, when Floyd was seventeen, he married his childhood sweetheart, Ruby Hargrove. He was ready to work but there just wasn't any work available. He left home to follow the wheat harvest, the only work he could find, but when the fall harvest was done, there was no work.

Desperate, Floyd at the age of eighteen purchased a pistol and held up a post office, taking all the postmaster's petty cash. The local sheriff soon arrested Floyd on suspicion of the robbery, but his father gave him an alibi.

On September 11, 1925, at age twenty-one, Floyd sat in the front seat of a Ford sedan. It was 6:50 a.m. The sedan was parked across the street from a Kroger food store main office building in St. Louis. Bill Miller, whom Floyd met in a local tavern, was an employee of Kroger and had laid out a payroll robbery plan. An occasional train whistle could be heard in the distance as they waited for the office manager to arrive. The manager showed up right on time.

The two hijackers pulled their hats low and charged across the street and through the office door before it could be closed. Floyd jerked the telephone line from the wall, then tied, gagged, and blindfolded the terrified office manager. Miller opened the safe and helped himself to the Kroger payroll. In less than ten minutes, they had $11,000 in canvas bags.

Having so much money paralyzed Floyd. He was afraid to take the money with him out onto the street, but he was also afraid to leave it in his room. He spent the entire early part of the morning dividing it into stacks then hiding the stacks, only to put them back on the bed to count them again. He didn't trust Bill Miller and the feeling was mutual.

Not far from his boarding house on King's Highway, there

was a Studebaker dealership. Floyd admired a robin's egg blue Studebaker with white leather interior and white sidewall tires. He began walking to the showroom every day just to look at that car. He thought about marching in and pricing it, but he felt his clothes were too shabby to be paying cash for a new car. He went to a nearby tailor shop and purchased a fashionable gray fedora hat, brown gabardine suit, a nice white shirt, a red tie, and a pair of black patent leather shoes. He couldn't resist a pair of black kid gloves. All dressed up and excited, his knees shaking, his courage began to wane. What if he asked the wrong question and they spotted him for a rube? Or what if they refused to sell him the car of his dreams?

Finally, he worked up his nerve and walked into the showroom and headed straight for the blue Studebaker. A salesman, a short stout fellow with a mustache, approached him. Floyd asked the price of the beautiful blue Studebaker. "Twelve hundred dollars," the salesman replied. Before Floyd could answer, the salesman touched the cuff of Floyd's suit. "Gabardine—can't afford it myself, but I know it when I see it—we have cheaper models of course if you are interested."

Nervous, Floyd pulled a roll of bills from his pocket and quickly counted out twenty-four fifty-dollar bills into open palm of the outstretched hand of the astonished salesman. A week earlier, he would never have dreamed that he would have twelve hundred dollars cash in his pocket.

Floyd had a few weeks of glorious living. Then the police arrived at his boarding house, arrested him for the Kroger job, and found some of the money hidden in his room. His cherished blue Studebaker was impounded, and he was sentenced to five years and hauled off to the huge Missouri State Penitentiary in Jefferson City, a pitiless old-fashioned "big house." There he was introduced to the leather lash, sweatbox, ball and chain, and sadistic guards. After three years of pure hell, he was paroled. He vowed he would never allow himself to be put in prison again.

Upon returning home to Hanson, Oklahoma, Floyd learned that his father had been shot and killed by Jim Mills, a moonshine competitor who had sworn a vendetta against the family. Floyd sat in the Sallisaw County courthouse and listened as Jim Mills was acquitted of the murder. He went home, loaded his rifle, and followed Mills into the nearby Cookston Hills. Jim Mills was never seen again.

Floyd left for Kansas City, a wide-open, anything-goes, no-holds-barred town, under the control of Tom Pendergast, politician and mob boss. It was there that he met Red Lovett, a fellow ex-convict. Lovett had a friend, Jim Bradley, who had a list of fat little banks in northern Ohio. The three men went to work and were doing quite well when they hit a snag. While making their get away from a robbery in Sylvania, Ohio, on March 11, 1930, they ran a red light and a patrol car gave chase. Bradley fired a machine gun from the backseat into the pursuing police car, wrecking it and killing Officer Harlan F. Maines. Lovett lost control of the getaway car and hit a telephone pole. The police pried the bank robbers from the wreckage.

They were tried and convicted for the murder of Officer Maines. Jim Bradley was sent to the electric chair, Red Lovett received life in prison, and Floyd faced the same stern judge and was sentenced to fifteen years in the Ohio State Prison.

Charles Arthur Floyd was not about to go back to prison. As a train transporting him roared through the night on May 25, 1930, Floyd felt like a caged animal. When his guards dozed off, he seized the opportunity to hurl himself through the train window. He hit the ground still handcuffed and tumbled through the darkness, then disappeared into a cornfield, making good his escape. Floyd made his way to the only place on earth where he knew he could find protection among the hill folks in Cookston County.

Meanwhile back in Texas, Governor Ross Sterling paroled Clyde Barrow, a convict spawned in the slums of West Dallas from the Huntsville prison. Clyde returned to Dallas, where he would form his own gang. The gang drove fast cars, carried machine guns, and robbed banks. Before his demise, Clyde Barrow and his gang would terrorize the Southwest—murdering fourteen people, nine of them lawmen.

The banks in Oklahoma practiced a tyranny of foreclosures. When a farmer asked for a loan to buy his seed for next year's crop, he would have to sign a hefty mortgage on his land for the seed money. If the crops failed, the bank would foreclose on the farm.

On Tuesday, November 1, 1932, a week before President Franklin Roosevelt was elected, the blue Studebaker rolled into Sallisaw, Oklahoma. With Floyd behind the wheel, Auzie Elliot in the front seat, and George Birdwell in the back, they came to rob the bank that had foreclosed on the Floyd family's farm a few years earlier.

At 9:00 a.m., Floyd parked across the street from the Sallisaw State Bank. He casually got out of the car, went into the barbershop with a machine gun cradled under his arm, and shook hands with everyone inside. He waved to some men who were lounging across the street and strolled toward the bank. Everyone in town had known he was coming.

"Howdy, Chock. What you doing in town?"

"How are you, Newt!" Floyd responded as he waved and winked, "I'm going to rob the bank!"

Floyd's grandfather, Earl Floyd, was sitting with two other toothless old-timers on a spit-and-whittle bench at the hardware store.

"Give 'em hell, Chock!"

"Grandpa! What are you doing here this time of day?"

"Come to see you rob the bank, Chock! I'll take a couple o' hundred if you got any leftover." chuckled Grandpa Floyd.

Charlene Gordon was the only teller on duty when he walked into the bank. He recognized her at once; he had seen her at parties and dances in town.

"Mornin', Charlene," Floyd said. "I'd be obliged if you would hand over the money as quick as possible."

Charlene stalled. "Aw, Chock—don't rob us! We're about to go under as it is."

His machine gun pointing harmlessly at the ceiling, Floyd raked all the bank's money into a sack as Charlene looked on, an unhappy expression on her face. Floyd asked, "Where are your farm loan files?"

Charlene pulled open a file drawer filled with liens. Floyd took the files, stuffed them into the potbellied stove, and watched while they burned.

"You know I'm a widow, Chock. If the bank fails and my kids go hungry, I'll curse your soul, Charles Floyd!"

"Charlene, if there is any trouble, just get in touch with Grandpa," Floyd told her. "I'll see that you don't suffer."

As Floyd stepped from the bank, he saw that Grandpa had fallen asleep. He stuffed a couple of $100 bills into the old man's shirt pocket. The other men watched and waved as the blue Studebaker drove out of sight.

A dark cloud was building over the business of bank-robbing. An organization called the Federal Bureau had structured a plan that squeezed the profit from it.

A list of all money delivered from the Federal Reserve to local banks was filed with the Federal Bureau. Now, when the banks were robbed, bills with registered numbers made a paper trail to the thieves.

The term "hot money" was used for the registered bills. Tom Pendergast, head of the Kansas City mob, made a market for hot money, twenty-five cents on the dollar. He banked the money in Switzerland and then made withdrawals in Swiss francs as needed. He was then able to convert the francs back into dollars at his bank in Kansas City.

Frank "Jelly" Nash, an insider who knew all about the Pendergast operation, had been captured in Hot Springs, Arkansas, early in 1933 and was serving a seven-year sentence for bank robbery. Tom Pendergast worried that Nash would trade what he knew for a reduced sentence. He got word to Nash to sit tight—he would get him out of jail.

Pendergast, through his Hot Springs police force connections, learned Jelly Nash was being transported to Kansas City on the Missouri Pacific Flyer. He awarded a lucrative contract on Nash's life to Solly Weissman, Adam Richetti, and Arthur "Pretty Boy" Floyd. They were paid to see that Nash never left Kansas City alive.

On a balmy spring, Saturday, June 17, 1933, a number of lawmen were waiting at the Kansas City railroad terminal to meet the Flyer and escort Jelly Nash to Leavenworth prison by car. Unnoticed by the lawmen, a green Chevrolet sedan pulled in and parked close by. Pretty Boy Floyd and Solly Weissman sat in the backseat, their machine guns held low out of sight. Vern Miller sat at the wheel, Adam Richetti was beside him, and two machine guns were tucked away in the front seat.

The killers watched the escort emerge with their captive. The lawmen paused briefly and saw nothing to arouse their suspicion. They escorted Nash toward the car, which was parked at the east terminal entrance.

A crowd of curious onlookers gathered as Bureau Agent Jim Lackey opened the right rear door, and Agent Frank Smith waited behind him. Both men were carrying shotguns.

Otto Reed, police chief of McAlester, Oklahoma, got in behind the wheel, while Nash was pushed into the front seat by a Kansas City police detective, Red Grooms. The green Chevrolet pulled out and moved toward the prison car. The shocked lawmen looked up to see men standing on the running board, holding machine guns pointed in their direction.

The spectators stood transfixed by the incredible scene. Red Grooms pulled his pistol and was able to squeeze off two shots before a deadly volley of machine gun bullets riddled the prison car and its helpless and unfortunate occupants.

Agent Caffrey fell to the concrete, dead. Chief Reed took

a chestful of bullets as Nash waved his manacled hands frantically at the shooters. "For God's sake!" he shouted, "Don't shoot me!" But the continued bursts of gunfire silenced him forever.

The top of his head was blown away. Bullets were bouncing on the concrete as they tore through the prone, dead victims.

Mary McElroy, daughter of the city manager, had inside information and had invited her boyfriend Blackie Audett to view the grizzly event. They watched from less than fifty yards away as the green Chevrolet sped from the murder scene. There was no pursuit—a rumor was later confirmed that Mary McElroy's father had helped orchestrate the plan.

With Prohibition and the Depression in full swing, the United States was experiencing the worst crime wave in its history. It was an era of notorious criminals—Al Capone, Machine Gun Kelly, Harvey Bailey, and John Dillinger. Now a new menace, the Barrow gang in West Dallas, was beginning to make headlines in the Southwest.

When news of the Kansas City massacre reached Washington, the new U.S. attorney general Homer Cummings said, "This constitutes an attack by the underworld on organized society; and we take this as their declaration of war, and a renaissance in law enforcement is about to take place."

Out of the bloodshed in Kansas City would arise the law enforcement agency that would be known as the Federal Bureau of Investigation. In 1908, Teddy Roosevelt had created a small branch of the federal government called the Bureau of Investigation, an organization of accountants and attorneys formed to delve into corporate records and monopolistic trusts. They were sometimes referred to as trustbusters.

A young zealot by the name of J. Edgar Hoover took over the agency in 1924. Hoover was furious over the murder of one of his agents, and he seized on this opportunity to demand an audience with Congress and newly elected President Franklin D. Roosevelt. He demanded that his men be allowed to carry arms and be given the authority to make arrests and cross state lines. Roosevelt, anxious to grab any kind of newspaper headlines that would take attention away from the misery of the Great Depression, gave Hoover his blessing to turn the newly formed Federal Bureau of Investigation into a ruthless, hard-hitting, crime-busting machine.

J. Edgar Hoover soon became the face of American crime fighting. He created a brotherhood of law enforcement officers across the United States. A list of the "Ten Most Wanted" criminals was compiled and became a regular feature of the agency's operation. The FBI's main thrust was always to apprehend whoever headed the list as Public Enemy Number One, and they methodically killed the most notorious outlaws in the United States.

The newspapers started picking up on the name of "G-men" (Government Men).[1] The legal execution of outlaws became so grizzly that the papers soon began referring to the G-men as "killers with badges."

End Note

1. A Kansas City bootlegger coined the term G-men when cornered by FBI agents holding machine guns. He shouted, "Don't shoot, G-men!"

HOWARD HUGHES AT THE DICE TABLE

IT WAS FIVE thirty, Sunday morning, September 27, 1929. Benny Binion sat at his desk on the second floor of the Southland Hotel in Dallas, counting the Saturday night take from his casino. His phone rang. The voice of Top O' Hill Casino's owner Fred Browning came over the wire.

"Benny, I'm glad I caught ya. I got a hot shooter at the Hill that's a half a million ahead and he wants to take the limit off an' roll for all of it."

Benny put his cigar down.

"Who's the pit, boss?"

"Benny Bickers."

"Do you know the shooter?"

Fred turned from the phone and asked his wife, Mary, "What's the kid's name?" Turning back to the phone, he said, "His name is Howard Hughes. He's building a movie theater in Oak Cliff."

"Has he had breakfast yet?" Benny asked.

"No," Fred replied.

"Tell him you're starved and break for breakfast," Benny said. "I'm gonna back you, but I want to make a phone call before I come out."

Benny dialed the home number of his friend Bill Decker, chief of criminal investigation with the Dallas County sheriff's department. Decker was a walking encyclopedia. Benny wanted to get a line on who he was going up against.

Benny could imagine Decker sitting on the side of his bed in his undershirt, needing a shave, his glass eye cocked and out of synch with the good one. Decker let out a low whistle as he repeated the name. "Howard Hughes—shooting for a half a million at the Hill. Yeah, Benny, Fred's got a live one. The kid's old man built an oil tool company in Houston and the kid is richer than nine miles up a mule's ass. Fred has a good one hooked if he doesn't get hooked himself."

Benny hung up the phone and hollered for his driver, a huge black man nicknamed Gold Dollar, to bring the car around. Then he opened his safe and told his associate John Bob Motley to put a million cash in a suitcase.

The black Cadillac roared across the Trinity River on the Oak Cliff viaduct, Gold Dollar driving, John Bob sitting next to him with a Thompson submachine gun cradled in his arms. Benny was smoking a cigar in the backseat, a sawed-off twelve-gauge shotgun across his knee. Gold Dollar turned right on the Turnpike and didn't stop for red lights or take his foot off the gas until the casino gates came into view. A guard waved them through. Benny looked at his watch. They had come the entire thirty-one miles in just over twenty minutes.

Benny's entourage made its way to the dining room accompanied by two of Fred's guards. Motley set the suitcase down on a table where Fred and Mary Browning were finishing breakfast. Across the table sat a good-looking young man in his early twenties and an attractive young blonde.

Fred introduced the young man as Howard Hughes and

his companion as Jean Harlow. After the introduction, Benny looked at Howard Hughes and said, "I understand you have had a good run of luck and want to do some serious gambling."

Hughes answered, "Beginner's luck, I guess."

Benny turned to Fred. "I want you to either close the game now, or if Howard wins on the next roll, put your casino on the line against Mr. Hughes's million dollars and the winner takes all."

Benny knew that by establishing rules before the dice started rolling, he had given Fred a good chance to get all his money back. Mary glanced nervously at Fred, who showed no emotion, and he simply nodded affirmatively. Benny knew two things: any time you interrupt a long-winning streak by taking a short break, it is always a mistake, and if the kid started losing and didn't show discipline, it could bring in a lot of money. Hughes took his place at the end of Fred's table and pushed all the chips to the line. Pit boss Benny Bickers sang out, "Half a million on the line!" Benny took the stick, toyed with eight dice, then cut out two of them and pushed them to Mr. Hughes.

Benny said, "A seven or an eleven on the first roll will be a winner. Good luck, sir!" Hughes picked up the dice, rolled them between his hands, and asked for a seven. The dice skittered down the green felt, hit the bumper, and came up a five and a six.

Benny sang out, "Eleven a winner!"

Jean Harlow squealed and clapped her hands. Gold Dollar moved the suitcase full of money to Hughes's end of the table.

Benny shoved the dice back to Hughes and said, "Good Luck, kid. You may be about to win Fred Browning's casino."

Hughes picked up the dice and held them for Harlow to kiss, then threw them down the table, and when they stopped spinning, an ace and a three showed. Benny held the dice for Hughes to see.

Benny sang out, "Four is the point, mark the four, four will be a winner on the line!" and shoved the dice back to the kid. Hughes picked them up and threw again; this time an ace and a deuce showed.

Benny chanted, "Three craps! All good shooters shoot craps!" He shoved the dice back to the kid.

Showing no emotion, Hughes picked up the dice. Mary stood stoically beside her husband. When four showed up as the point, Fred stood a little straighter. Benny calculated to himself *that the odds were now almost eighty percent in Browning's favor that the kid would seven out now.* Hughes threw the dice two more times. On the third roll, Benny sang out, "Seven a loser, it's all away!"

Jean Harlow, in disbelief, uttered an unladylike profanity. Hughes's expression never changed. Benny now realized that money had no meaning for Hughes, that it was the thrill of the game and the heady sensation of temporary control that had brought him to this casino's table.

TOP O' HILL HEIST

THE KANSAS CITY mob had a map of underground railroads all across the United States with rendezvous locations and safe houses along the way. Their well-organized bank-robbing was like an intricately planned hard-hitting military operation.

Vern Miller, the wheelman at the Kansas City massacre, chose to move north and west from the murder scene. The police had trailed Miller to his hideout but found only bloody rags indicating that Kansas City Police Detective Red Grooms's pistol shots had found their mark.

Miller's naked, mangled body was found later in a ditch near Detroit on November 29, 1933. His death had all the earmarks of mob retaliation. It appeared that red-hot flatirons had scorched his skin. He was tied up head to toe, and ice picks had been used to puncture his cheeks and tongue.

Two weeks after the discovery of Miller's corpse, Solly Weissman's body was found in the same condition on the outskirts of Chicago. It was now apparent to police that both men had been killed to silence them. They were two of the alleged assassins of Jelly Nash, kingpin of the Pendergast money-laundering operation.

The police surmised that it was impossible that the shooters at the Kansas City massacre did not recognize Nash; he had been placed in the front seat and was waving his manacled hands, pleading not to be shot. The killing was simply a mob hit; Nash had been marked for death and the killers had been paid a handsome sum to take him out. Once he had been assassinated, his killers in turn were being murdered to silence them. But what happened to the other shooter? Where was Pretty Boy Floyd?

When the green Chevrolet sedan left the Kansas City crime scene, the first stop was Vern Miller's rooming house to pick up some first-aid medicine and bandages. Miller's wounds were diagnosed by an underground doctor as not being serious. The green Chevrolet then proceeded to a wrecking yard on the east side of town where each shooter picked up his own car; the Chevrolet disappeared forever into the bowels of the Kansas City wrecking yard.

Floyd headed south toward Oklahoma and the roads and safe houses he knew well. The other two shooters headed toward their own territory. Floyd realized that the law would anticipate his appearance in Oklahoma, so he continued south to Dallas.

The Red Brick Hotel in West Dallas was at the center of a squalid sixteen-square-mile sanctuary for desperadoes and outlaws known as the Devil's Back Porch. Only a short distance from downtown, it was a no-man's-land in Dallas County outside the city limits where the city police had no jurisdiction.

The Devil's Back Porch was located on the west bank of the Trinity River and was connected to downtown by the Continental Street viaduct. Today the street that was the spine of the Devil's Back Porch is Singleton Boulevard. In 1933, the name of the street was Eagle Ford Road, named for the ford crossing of the Trinity before the viaduct was built.

Every street that crossed Eagle Ford Road had a name, but there were no street signs. None of the streets were paved and few even had gravel. Desperate people lived wherever they could set up shelter. There was no city water and no indoor plumbing. The families lived in huts and lean-tos; some lived in the dump just across the bridge where wagons disposed of the city's garbage, and hungry children would scramble over the stinking hills of refuse looking for something to eat.

A huge cement plant once occupied adjacent territory. Dallas had an unquenchable appetite for cement used to build the (then) world's largest concrete structure, the Oak Cliff viaduct over the Trinity River, in 1912. In the 1920s, the Dallas skyline was impressive with the Adolphus Hotel, the Magnolia Building, and the Praetorian Building—all jewels in its crown.

With the stock market crash in 1929, the Dallas building boom came to a halt. The cement company abandoned the Devil's Back Porch. The earth was scarred with pits where tons of limestone had been quarried for cement. Stagnant water filled the huge holes gouged in the earth.

Half the typhoid and nearly all the county's tuberculosis came from this filthy, polluted, and contaminated area. Many families had several children and two or three dogs. There were no dogcatchers and no truant officers, and it was like a war zone, evoking the survival of the fittest.

Some of the Southwest's most notorious gangs and killers were spawned in West Dallas during the twenties and thirties. The Red Brick Hotel, at the intersection of Eagle Ford Road and Vilbig Street, was the citadel of the outlaw stronghold.

A barbershop and dance hall were located on the ground floor. The hotel smelled of cigarette smoke, beer, and barbecue served from behind a bar in the dance hall. A notorious flyer named Slats Rodgers was known to land and take off on Vilbig Street right next to the hotel.

On more than one occasion, this rogue pilot transported the Barrow gang to and from their Louisiana hideout when after fourteen murders they were really hot and had to stay out of sight while things cooled down.

When Bonnie Parker read about the Kansas City massacre in the Dallas papers and saw Pretty Boy Floyd's picture, she made a connection—he was her kind of guy. Bonnie asked Floyd Hamilton, Clyde Barrow's liaison and the older brother of Raymond Hamilton, who had been dubbed the Blond Bandit from West Dallas, to talk with Floyd and invite him to run with the Barrow gang.

Hamilton had learned by the grapevine that Floyd was in town at the Red Brick Hotel. When the two men met, Floyd rejected Bonnie's idea out of hand, saying Clyde Barrow was a mad-dog killer and not making enough money for what he did. Raymond Hamilton returned to Bonnie and simply said that Pretty Boy Floyd was not interested in joining the Barrow gang. He thought it best not to pass the gratuitous insult on to Clyde Barrow's mall.

Bonnie did not give up her idea. She went to the Red Brick Hotel and waited for Pretty Boy Floyd. When he came in to have lunch, she approached his table and flirtatiously asked if she could join him. Floyd had a way with women and instantly had Bonnie's afternoon all planned for her.

One pint of Four Roses and three breathless hours later, Bonnie revealed her true identity. She also revealed information about a half-million-dollar heist and repeated to Floyd that Clyde was a mad-dog killer and was poorly paid for the heat he had brought on himself and the gang with his senseless killings. And then she described the vault at the Top O' Hill Casino. "The hundred-dollar bills are wired together in bales so big that they the men sometimes use them as chairs!" she exclaimed. "They have to use a wagon and a wheelbarrow to move those bales of money around!"

Taking a deep pull on her cigarette and exhaling slowly, she said, "And on weekends, it is not unusual for a cash flow of a half a million dollars to accumulate in that casino vault!"

Pretty Boy Floyd decided he would play along and told Bonnie that he recognized that she had brains, but he wanted to control the heist and Clyde would either have to go to the back of the boat and sit down or be killed. Bonnie felt herself flushing and her heart pounding. This was exactly the response she had anticipated and hoped for.

She would later conspire with Clyde, convincing him to go along with the plan. Then she would whisper to him that after they made their score, they would eliminate Pretty Boy Floyd once and for all.

Harvey Bailey was raised a farm boy in Sullivan County, Missouri, and was a World War I army veteran. At age forty-five, Bailey was a massive, intimidating man, a criminal mastermind, and small-arms expert, who was sometimes referred to as "the professor of appraisal of goods and opportunities."

Bailey's activities as a bank robber were the most profitable of any outlaw of the era. He would enter a town and read the financial statements of the banks, paying special attention to the first item listed—cash. Once he found a bank he considered worth his time, he continued to research what he called the special risk factor.

He would then determine the number of employees and guards and make a map of several different escape routes with a designated preferred route and always an alternate escape plan.

Bailey kept a manifest of available gang members in any given geographical area. He always struck with sufficient firepower and fast automobiles, and he was suspected to have been the architect of the Kansas City massacre.

Pretty Boy Floyd placed a call to the switchboard where

Harvey Bailey had a shapely brunette screen his calls. Floyd left a cryptic message about the price of eggs on the Chicago Commodity Exchange. When Bailey returned the call, Floyd didn't mention Top O' Hill Casino, but told Bailey he needed tear gas canisters for a bank job. He knew Bailey would not be interested in a bank job because the hot money exchange cut too deep into the profit.

Bailey responded, "There are tear gas canisters for the taking in the National Guard Armory at Ranger, Texas. J. L. Ford, an old army buddy of mine, is in charge of ordinance. I'll talk to him and see what his price will be. I'll get back to you tomorrow at noon."

Later the next day, Bailey called back. "The deal is set. Ford wants to make it look like a burglary. You will receive a price list for machine guns, automatic weapons, and the canisters. Your boys can take whatever they need. Be sure to take the money to Ford first—don't make him come to you to collect!"

As he drove through the night toward Ranger, Clyde Barrow was pleased with the idea of hitting the National Guard Armory. The Hamilton brothers were with him. Clyde's only reservation was that he didn't like leaving Bonnie behind in Dallas. He didn't trust her with Pretty Boy Floyd in town.

After the armory job, Clyde made reservations at the Top O' Hill Casino for himself, the Hamilton brothers, and Pretty Boy Floyd. They were going to the casino to case it.

Later when they were in the casino, Pretty Boy Floyd saw Mugsy Mitchell and Roscoe McClung, both ex-cons he knew from the Missouri State Penitentiary. Mugsy was working as a dice dealer. Floyd and Mugsy exchanged a high sign they had used in prison.

Floyd crooked his finger over his nose; Mugsy responded by tugging at his ear. When Mugsy was relieved at the dice table, Floyd followed him outside for a smoke. Mugsy smiled and said, "You're here with the Barrow gang casing Fred's casino."

Grinning, Floyd responded, "You're a bright boy, Mugsy. We need an inside man and a map."

The tip of Mugsy's cigarette glowed as he took a deep pull. "Fred Browning has been awful good to me. What's my help worth?"

"Ten percent for you and Roscoe McClung," Floyd answered.

Mugsy remained silent, deep in thought, until he replied, "Fred Browning is paying us well. I couldn't get a job like this anywhere else." His cigarette sailed into the darkness, sparkling as it spiraled out of sight.

Floyd responded, "On New Year's Eve night, we figure the vault will have a half a million or more in it." He continued, "All you have to do is be sure it's not locked and you'll have fifty thousand or more to split with McClung."

Mugsy started laughing and could hardly contain himself.

Floyd asked, "What's so damn funny?"

Regaining his composure, Mugsy said, "Well, Fred, ain't been that good to me! Tell me where you're staying and I'll bring you the map."

After casing the casino, the newly formed gang had a party at the Adolphus Hotel. When they had finished a sumptuous meal, they took the elevator to the presidential suite. Over brandy and cigars, Pretty Boy Floyd explained his plan. They would make the heist on New Year's Eve just at the stroke of twelve. The crap tables would have done their job of taking most of the money from the patrons' pockets. Gas masks would be concealed under specially tailored dress coats. "It should be a walk in the park," Raymond Hamilton said as he drained his glass.

On New Year's Eve 1933, a stream of headlights like glittering stars in the dark of night appeared on the old Fort Worth Turnpike, their destination the exclusive Top O' Hill Casino. Each car was stopped at the gate tower, and the casino guards checked the occupant's identification and placed a pass under the windshield wiper. Bumper to bumper, Cadillacs, Lincolns, Stutz Bearcats, and even a beautiful Duisenberg Phantom came winding up the tree-lined drive to the casino entrance where guards double-checked the windshield passes, then parked the cars.

Glamorous, beautifully gowned women and their tuxedoed escorts were welcomed for an evening of elegant dining and dancing to the sounds of a big-name band—and of course to try their luck at the roulette wheels, the dice, or blackjack tables.

The heist went as planned. The tear gas took out all resistance. The vault at Top O' Hill was cleaned out. The money was loaded into a Ford panel truck that Clyde Barrow had stolen only hours earlier. At 12:36 a.m., over a half million in cash rolled through the night—Clyde Barrow at the wheel, Pretty Boy Floyd riding shotgun. The two Hamilton brothers followed closely behind in their car.

There was no pursuit. The truck rumbled through the dark downtown streets, then turned left on Maple Avenue, and into the underground parking garage of Dallas's Stoneleigh Hotel. The Ford panel truck pulled in and parked in a reserved slot with pickup trucks waiting on each side. By prior arrangement, the money was to be divided equally, loaded into each truck, covered and secured under a canvas tarpaulin.

Pretty Boy Floyd would go his way with half the loot, and the Barrow gang would go their way with the other half.

Bonnie Parker had two plans; Pretty Boy Floyd would kill Clyde and the Hamilton brothers in the basement of the Stoneleigh, or the other was an agreement with Clyde Barrow to kill Pretty Boy Floyd.

None of her sinister plans would however materialize. Moments after the casino was hit, the owner Fred Browning called Benny Binion. His eyes still smarting from the lingering tear gas, Fred Browning explained to Benny they had just been hit for a half a million or more.

Binion made two phone calls. The first was to Deputy Sheriff Bill Decker who was in charge of criminal investigation.[1] Decker had just got to sleep when his phone rang. He cursed, turned on the light, and sat up in bed. His glass eye stared back at him from a glass of water on the nightstand.

Binion hurriedly told Decker about the casino heist, and Decker instructed him to send his men to the Stoneleigh Hotel. One of Decker's snitches had told him that he had heard of a possible heist at the Top O' Hill and a plan to transfer the loot into two getaway trucks parked in the hotel's underground garage.

Decker mused that if his information was correct, Fred Browning would have his money back by sunup. Before the Barrow gang could transfer the stolen money to the trucks in the Stoneleigh's garage, Benny Binion and six of his men appeared as if by magic from behind parked cars, shotguns in hand.

Bonnie knew her bloodthirsty plans were about to be aborted when she heard Benny Binion bellow, "If anyone so much as bats an eye, you're all dead meat! Before you took Fred Browning's money, we was all friends! Now I'm gonna take Fred's money back to him. And you folks can get out of town, or I can drop you right here!"

He continued, "Put your guns on the floor and get in your car and leave. We can still be friends and you'll owe me a favor." The guns clattered to the concrete floor and the outlaws left, glad to be alive.

Bill Decker's phone rang again and Binion told him the story of the thwarted robbery without revealing any names. He invited Decker to show up at Top O' Hill for an evening out. Tommy Dorsey's band was playing. Decker laughed, hung up the phone, and crawled back into bed beside his beautiful redheaded wife, Cecil.

DALLAS: THE LITTLE MONTE CARLO ON THE TRINITY

In 1934, Joe Civello, the Dallas Mafia don, attended a meeting of all Mafia chieftains from major cities in Chicago chaired by Sam Giancana, who took Al Capone's seat at the head of the syndicate table when Capone went to jail for income tax evasion in 1931. Each Don was making a report on money-making opportunities in his city for the mob.

When Joe's turn to speak came, he said, "Dallas is like a ripe hanging tomato, even though our country is in a great depression, my city did eighteen million dollars in gambling and prostituting last year. Benny Binion has twenty-seven casinos within a two-mile square area of downtown. People are calling Dallas the Little Monte Carlo on the Trinity. If you want to take a drink, gamble, or get laid, Dallas is the place to go." He continued, "But now is not a good time to move on Dallas, because Benny Binion is boss. He is smart, tough, and he has some ex–Texas Rangers on his payroll that are dangerous killers."

148

Sam Gincanna, head of the Mafia syndicate, wisely chose to wait and not try to take over Dallas under Binion's watch.

At this time in our history, Tom Potter, a wealthy east Texas oil man, had moved to Dallas from Kilgore. Oil was discovered on his property and they drilled wells all over it. He bought a fine house on Swiss Avenue here in Dallas.

When Franklin D. Roosevelt came to Dallas for the opening of the Texas Centennial, he rode in Mr. Potter's yellow Packard convertible. In 1936, during the Texas Centennial, a lot of the East Texas oil people were moving to Dallas and they had a lot of new money. They seemed determined to just throw it away, and Dallas gamblers were just as determined to accommodate.

Ben Whitaker refurbished his Whitmore hotel just for the centennial crowd and the new Texas oil rich. That hotel was so sophisticated for its time it had ceiling fans in every room, secret tunnels and passageways so you could go from one place to another without being seen.

Whitaker was the Dallas gambling syndicate boss and there were several different gambling operations that had divided the city into territories controlled by a boss that reported to Whitaker. Fred Merrill was Whitaker's enforcer and worked out all the grievances and territorial disputes. He had his own casino in Rockwall just outside the city limits and lived just behind H. L. Hunts's place on the west shore of White Rock Lake. He had quite a bit of influence with the Dallas police department, and anyone that didn't abide by the syndicate's rules found themselves in trouble with the police department. There was the Binion gang, they hung out around the Southland Hotel and had a continuous dice game in room 222. They were referred to as the Southland gang. Ivy Miller had North Dallas, and his gang was called the Miller gang.

Benny Bickers Sr. had a club called the University Club in a penthouse on top of the Santa Fe Building. He said he would never take a drink before five o'clock but he had a watch that had nothing but fives on it. Herbert Noble had a downtown club called the Airmen's Club on Ivey Street. John Clark, *Honest John*, worked with Benny Binion running the casino in the Black Stone Hotel—when Benny left for Vegas, John went with him.

Tom Ramsay told of his father, Roy Ramsay, who ran a bust-out poker game in the Baker Hotel; Roy had a man in the hallway with a shotgun, and when the game was over, the bagman walked ahead unarmed while a guard was behind him with the shotgun as they transported the money to Binion's safe just down the street in the Southland Hotel.

Poker was a big thing back then, and a fellow by the name of Judge Earhart bankrolled the Cipango Club down on Tuttle Creek, where the Mansion stands today. That was on Ivy Miller's turf, and Miller furnished dealers for the big bust-out poker games. Ladies of the night worked the casino and took their Johns to convince rooms for a quick tryst. Eddie Zimmerman was the club manager.

There was an area in the bar that was wall-to-wall slot machines in the club. Slot machines were the real winners, and you could make more money than you can imagine from one slot machine. When the police would come through the front door to raid the club, there were panels that would come down hiding the slot machines. The police never did find the right way to get to the casino upstairs. A lot of Dallas property changed hands upstairs at that Cipango Club high-dollar poker table.

There was a hangar at Love Field called Littlefoots' Flying Service on Lemmon Avenue. That's where Jimmy Landrum, a Dallas high roller, had his airplane. H. L. Hunt had his plane in Littlefoots' hangar; you could hear him laugh and holler when they had the radio tuned to the horse races across the country and his horse came in.

The gamblers were all making good money and they were looking for something to do, and they learned to fly and they bought all kinds of airplanes. Now they were flying around in their new plane with a pocketful of money having a great time.

Some of these gamblers who had some flying experience joined the Air Force when the war started. James R. Cobb Jr. was an army air corps cadet when he met these men and learned that the older men ferrying military planes were connected to gamblers, some old barnstormers and some crop dusters. There were some exciting poker games that went on at that time, and the old pilots talked about pilots like Major Bill Long, Salts Rodgers, and how they made a living barnstorming during the twenties and early thirties while other pilots were all starving to death.

Gambling was the number one industry in Dallas, and on more than one occasion, when someone from out of town tried to open shop without paying dues to the Dallas gambling syndicate, there was a killing.

A TRAGEDY FOR THE
BINION FAMILY

IT WAS ONE of those beautiful, bright, shiny Texas winter afternoons, January 10, 1934. Jack Binion decided he would check in at Love Field. It was always a great way to spend some time. He soon spotted some friends—Walter "Tige" A. Flowers, thirty, and his mechanic Oscar V. Poynter, fourty. They were tuning the engine of Tige's new Stinson high-wing monoplane.

Flowers had held a commercial transport pilot's license since 1928. He was a veteran pilot with over 1,100 hours logged. Flowers had been the object of national publicity when he and a companion crashed in the jungles of Nicaragua. Suffering from the crash and lost, the two men persevered and found their way back to civilization. Flower's mission had been to chart air routes through South America.

Jack knew both men and was always curious about motors, and especially airplane motors. He watched and helped when he could. After almost two hours of tinkering, Oscar listened to

152

the engine, wiped his hands, and was satisfied. The beautiful winter afternoon with its cool tranquil air beckoned the men and Tige filed a flight plan. Jack took the copilot's seat, while Tige flew. Oscar came along as the flight engineer; he wanted to savor the performance of his handiwork and he loved to listen to the big engine roar.

The sun was poised on the horizon, it was 5:15 p.m. Jim Ryan, the watchman at the White Rock Pump Station, on the shore of White Rock Lake just outside the city limits of Dallas, and about fifteen miles from Love Field, heard the roar of a low-flying airplane. He left his office and went topside to get a better look. When he arrived, he saw a Stinson barreling through some trees in the J. W. Morris's yard about fifteen feet off the ground headed for the lake.

The plane swung south along the shoreline, freighting a flock of ducks into the air. Flashing back across the dam, the plane swung to approach the lake again, its wheels barely clearing the water. As it sped along the eastern shore of the lake, ducks scrambled to get out of the way.

The plane slipped, and the right wing dipped into the lake water as the pilot attempted a turn to tight. A loud crack was heard as the plane's wing ripped off. Traveling at such a high speed, the airplane's fuselage flipped upside down, and with a huge splash, the ship plunged into fifteen feet of water. The force of the impact dislodged the engine from the plane and it catapulted into the mud and was buried at the bottom of the lake. The wing remained on the surface of the lake, with the tail structure sticking out.

A city truck with a wench attached a cable to the wreckage. They were able to pull the aircraft on shore and the bodies of Tige Flowers and Jack Binion were found still strapped in their seats.

Dallas police detective Lieutenant Will Fritz at Love Field examined the flight plan book for the plane. The logbook revealed that Walter "Tige" A. Flowers was the pilot, while Jack

Binion sat in the copilot's seat. The body of Oscar V. Poynter who appeared in the logbook had not been recovered with the wreckage.

Fritz returned to the scene and dispatched a rescue boat with firemen and grappling equipment. Even though the search was in the darkness of night, the body of Poynter was found in about an hour later not far from the point of impact of the aircraft. Upon examination of the bodies, all three men were pronounced dead. It was believed that they died instantly as all three had severe head injuries.

THE TEXAS CENTENNIAL

IT WAS IN February 1935 when Mr. Robert Thornton, a prominent Dallas banker who was also president of the Chamber of Commerce, called on Benny Binion in his office at room 222 in the Southland Hotel.

Thornton explained to Binion that Texas was going to have a centennial celebration in 1936 and that Dallas, Houston, San Antonio, and Fort Worth were in a pissing contest to see who could raise the most money because the federal government would match the funds of the city with the most money on the table.

Benny listened politely, and when Thornton finished, he asked, "Why have you come to me, how can I make a buck out of a centennial celebration in Dallas?"

Thornton replied, "Because four million people will pass through the gates of a centennial here in Dallas. The hotels and restaurants will be filled and business will boom."

"How much money did you have in mind as my part?" Binion asked.

"Two million would clinch the deal for Dallas."

A long silence followed, then Binion spoke slowly, "And the State Fairgrounds have four gates, right?"

"That's right, Benny."

Excited, Benny said, "Let me put a tractor trailer rig at each gate with a dice table inside and I'll come with the two million."

Tractor trailers were parked at each of the centennial gates. An Egyptian pyramid with palm trees, a crescent moon, and a camel were painted on the sides of the trailers.

A circus barker in a red striped shirt with a flat-brimmed straw hat stood outside hawking the temple of fate.

A Dallas policeman stood guard as people came and left the Texas Centennial while the barker chanted, "If you haven't been inside, you may never know what fortune and fate may have in store for you and your family."

A young stockbroker, Jim Gatewood Sr. (the author's father), who worked for Rauscher Pierce on the second floor of the Magnolia Building downtown Dallas, flanked by two other brokers, Dick Scott and Bill Hobbs, entered Benny's tractor trailer rig at the west gate of the centennial.

My father described the events that followed to me. "I had a good day in the market and was fifty dollars ahead. I decided to try my luck, and if I lost the fifty dollars, that would be my stop loss for Benny's game and it wouldn't ruin my day."

At that time in our life, Dad drove a model A Ford and we were paying seven dollars a month for a frame home with a two-acre onion patch on Bank Head Highway in Garland, Texas (now named North Garland Avenue), where the Catholic Church stands. Dad came home that afternoon with two grocery sacks full of money.

He dumped the money on the bed while he and my mother sang, "We're in the Money." I was in the second grade at the time and learning to count by fives. All the five-dollar bills were pushed to the head of the bed and it was my job to count them into neat stacks of twenty. It was only a few days after my seventh birthday and it seemed to take forever to count all those five-dollar bills. Dad had dumped a little over eleven thousand dollars on that bed.

My father told me it was just one of those things that seldom happen. He said he could do no wrong that day in Benny's game, he would get a five for a point and ask the dice for a five right back and get it. When the pit boss announced that the bank was broke and the game was closed, Dad offered to shoot for the tractor trailer rig, but the pit boss refused.

Dad had borrowed money from Jimmy Lang, a Dallas florist, to purchase the old Holley farm on Duck Creek, which was on a dirt wagon road two miles from the small farming community Rose Hill, Texas.

The money he won that day allowed him to pay off the note on the farm. I well remember that he and my mother burned the mortgage in the front yard of the frame home on the newly acquired land.

Gamblers know that the moral to this story is, *No-limit crap games are not a one-way street.*

BEN WHITAKER, DALLAS GAMBLING SYNDICATE BOSS

THE ORREN W. Whitaker family name appears in the 1910 Dallas census indexes with a Beckley Street address in Oak Cliff. Benjamin F. Whitaker is the fourth child born. He will be later known as Ben F. Whitaker and would, in Benny Binion's words, *have Dallas*.

> Johnny Scott, whose family owned and ran Scott's Sandwich Stand where the local high school students hung out, remembered Ben Whitaker. "He got his hair cut at Green's Barbershop down on the old Garland square. He always wore cowboy boots and drove a Lincoln Zephyr."

Will Fritz got a phone call from Ben Whitaker. "Your presence at my BBQ Saturday would add luster to the affair. Several of your friends will be there. Be sure and bring your

Thompson with you." Will agreed to attend the BBQ, which was held at Whitaker's ranch in Garland.

Dallas County Sheriff Smoot Smith and Chief Deputy Bill Decker were among the guests. While the ranch cadre put the finishing touches on the BBQ being prepared lakeside, Whitaker took the group on a tour of his horse stables, the exercise track, and a nine-hole golf course that he had laid out behind his two-story white-framed ranch house.

As the group toured the ranch, Whitaker explained, "The ranch was originally an eight-hundred-acre tract of land owned by W. R. 'Will' Kingsley who liked to be referred to as Colonel Kingsley.

"He always wore a white suit and a wide-brimmed white hat. Originally, the ranch had a wagon trail running through it that would later be named Kingsley Road after Colonel Kingsley.

"Colonel Kingsley had purchased the land to raise cotton. When the cotton market got soft, he sold the south half of the ranch to Randolph Caldwell. The part we're on now is what Mr. Caldwell purchased."

> Joseph Caldwell, Randolph Caldwell's surviving son, 3621 Cornell Drive, Dallas, Texas, reflected, "Back in the '30s, Dad sold or traded one-half of the ranch on the south side of Kingsley Road to a fellow named Ted Monroe, a Dallas criminal attorney. There was a beautiful white house on the crown of a wooded hill overlooking a man-made lake and a large red horse barn. Monroe later sold the property to Ben Whitaker, who kept a lot of his racehorses there. I remember meeting Whitaker one time when I was a little kid. He talked about putting his horses in all the important races, but I don't remember much about him other than that."

Ben Whitaker continued, "Now the reason I've asked Will Fritz and Bill Decker to bring their machine guns is because I have an old stump that's in the way of an exercise track that I'm building for my horses. I thought it would add luster to our party if the two lawmen would dig the stump out with their machine guns." Decker and Fritz stood toe to toe, the muzzles of their machine guns pointed at the old tree stump.

What Whitaker hadn't told Decker or Fritz was that Deputy Bill Wiseman, the demolition expert for the Dallas County sheriff's department, had put a half-pint whiskey bottle with some nitroglycerin at the base of the stump. A cheer went up as the stump was destroyed with a loud bang. The BBQ was served and the politicians began their politicking.

BILL DECKER, CHIEF DEPUTY IN CHARGE OF CRIMINAL INVESTIGATION SEARCHED FOR BETTY STEVENS

IF YOU WERE a Dallas power broker, judge, politician, con man, or gambler, Bill Decker knew about the backroom deals, bribes, and family problems. He was a walking encyclopedia of information gained because he was one of the most accommodating and clever politicians to ever walk the streets of Dallas.

His vast manifest of information came from his almost Chaplin-like concern for the inmates of the Dallas County jail. Many of the unfortunate incarcerated prisoners remember a mild-mannered deputy who visited them while they were in the depth of despair.

Decker would spend his spare time reading the arrest reports and then canvassing the new inmates. He was a chain-smoker, and his first question was always, "Do you need cigarettes?" His second question would always be, "Is there a friend or member of your family you would like to contact?" He would listen sympathetically to the prisoner's story and offer to get and recommend legal counsel.

He had a certain swagger and a talent for making the ladies of the horizontal trade bond with him and feel that they had made a true friend. Decker observed that privileged information about politicians, gang members, police charters, and gamblers was the favorite topic that scarlet ladies passed among themselves while detained.

Betty Stevens, who had been in and out of the county jail for pandering, had worked out an agreement with the management of the Bryan Street hotel, whereby she could accommodate a request for female companionship in her room on the hotel's second floor by appointment. She was dating a kingpin in the Dallas drug trade that beat her savagely and threatened to wash her face with battery acid.

Before her bruises healed and while she was still walking hunched over from the pain of broken ribs, a young FBI agent called on her, but she didn't tell him anything. She made up with the drug lord that had beaten her and he didn't have enough sense to keep his mouth shut. Betty learned most of the mob's trade secrets and passed them on to her new John, the young FBI agent. What followed was a large drug bust in Dallas and Betty Stevens disappeared.

No one thought much about Betty's disappearance. Ladies in her trade often moved to other cities without much fanfare. Benny heard a disturbing story and called his friend Sheriff Bill Decker and asked him to check with Jetty Bass for more accurate information.

Bass's real name was George Washington Bass. His brother was Christopher Columbus Bass. Jetty was half Comanche Indian and half Italian with coal-black hair. He stood a little over six feet tall, well-built and extremely handsome. When Jetty smiled, a set of perfect white teeth added to his charm. He was an excellent golfer and played all the Dallas and Ft. Worth country clubs. Jetty made love to most of his golf partner's wives and eventually got around to stealing their jewelry. He always left a playing card, the King of Hearts, when he took their jewelry. Everyone suspected who it was, but could not prove it.

Jetty owned a tavern, The Last Chance, on the Ft. Worth turnpike just outside of Arcadia Park. It was about four o'clock in the afternoon when Decker's red Oldsmobile pulled in and parked at the back of Jetty's tavern.

The smell of stale beer and cigarette smoke met Decker as he entered the dimly lit tavern. Decker blinked his one good eye to adjust for the darkness and took a seat at the bar in the corner where he could observe the afternoon's activity.

Hazel Murphy, whom Decker recognized as a working girl, came to the bar and asked, "What would you like this afternoon, Sheriff?" Hazel's remark indicated more than refreshment was available. Decker smiled; he understood.

"Is Jetty in?"

"Yeah, he's in the back."

"Bring me some coffee, Hazel, and tell Jetty I'm here."

Hazel disappeared into the kitchen. A customer came in and sat at the other end of the bar just as Jetty came down the hall from his office.

Jetty walked directly to the stranger at the bar. From behind the bar, Jetty leaned toward him and said, "I don't know you, the only people that are welcome here are people I know, and most of them are ex-convicts or outlaws. We talk business in here and you are not welcome!"

Jetty turned and served the customer a beer. "You get one beer, it's on the house, but when you finish it, leave and don't come back!"

Jetty turned toward Decker and motioned toward his office. They entered a small office with a desk and a couple of chairs with an ashtray on a desk overflowing with cigarette stubs and ashes.

"It's good to see you, Sheriff. What can I help you with this afternoon?"

"Jetty, I'm looking for a girl named Betty Stevens. Can you help me?"

Jetty rose, went to his office door, and shut it. He stood deep in thought, his back to the door, his hand on the doorknob.

"Damn, Decker, that's a grim story, it comes from the street. I can't vouch for it, but I'll tell you what I heard. Betty Stevens came to town about four years ago. She was one of those girls that show up in the bus station, bewildered and lost. She was picked up by a pimp and told the usual lies. When he got tired of her, she was passed around and ravished by the gang. They got her hooked on heroin and she wound up working out of the Bryan Street hotel. It was business as usual until she got in a fight with one of the dope dealers.

"He beat her badly and left her in the street. Before her bruises had healed and while she was still walking hunched from broken ribs, a young FBI agent called on her, but she didn't tell him anything. He left his card and told her to call if he could help her in any way.

"The story goes that she made up with the dope peddler that had beaten her. He didn't have enough sense to keep his mouth shut and she learned most of the mob's trade secrets and passed them on with anonymous phone calls to the young FBI agent.

"As you know, the largest drug bust in the history of Texas went down. The Dallas kingpins of the drug trade got jail time. Some of the Galveston boys came to town to reconstruct the local drug routes and deal some justice.

"Betty Stevens was put on the spot. A meeting of the local survivors of the drug bust was called in a vacant warehouse with a loft. There were about thirty of them. They took their seats in a small room. Centered at the other end of the room was a table and a full-length mirror on an elevated stage. The lighting had been arranged so the audience was in the dark and had a clear view.

"An ambulance pulled up outside the warehouse. A lady in a wheelchair was wheeled to the freight elevator, brought up, and pushed to the center of the stage by two men dressed in doctor's white jackets. She was a pretty lady, her face was made up, and her hair had just been done.

"A bright light from the ceiling illuminated Betty Stevens seated in her wheelchair. She was heavily sedated and groggy but conscious. The men dressed as doctors placed tourniquets just above her wrists and ankles. Another man pushed in a gurney with some tools.

"The first doctor asked Betty to blink her eyes once if she could see herself in the mirror. Betty blinked her eyes in response. He then admonished her for doing a terrible and unforgivable thing and again asked her to blink her eyes if she understood. Betty blinked her eyes once.

"He explained, so that others could learn from her mistake that she had to be made an example of because she had broken their code. 'Do you understand?' Betty blinked once.

"A voice from the audience called, 'You're in big trouble now, bitch!' There was a subdued murmur from the crowd.

"The first doctor nodded and the tourniquets on her ankles were tightened. Betty's ankle was placed inside the jaws of a heavy bolt cutter taken from the gurney. As the handles were pushed together, there was the sickening sound of bones snapping. The main bone of the left ankle was cut. The assembly gasped. Betty flinched but she did not cry out. The doctor slowly and deliberately amputated both her feet. The stumps of Betty's legs were dipped into bowls of tar and there was no loss of blood.

"The doctor held Betty's feet in front of her and asked, 'Do you see these feet? They are your feet! They are going to be dropped into the Trinity River!' Betty blinked once and dropped her head.

"The doctor began tightening the tourniquets on Betty's wrists. Again the bolt cutter severed her hands from her arms at the wrist. Bandages dipped in tar were wrapped around Betty's stumped arms. The doctor waved Betty's hands back and forth in front of her face as the other doctor held her head by her hair upright so she could see her hands.

"When the doctor holding Betty's hands asked her, did she recognize her hands, Betty blinked once, tears streaming down both her cheeks. He told her, 'Your hands will be buried in a West Dallas gravel pit. Your head is going to be cut off and thrown from Oak Cliff viaduct into the Trinity River. What is left of your body will be stripped and left in the city dump for flies and maggots to eat on it until it is beyond recognition.'

"The doctor moved behind Betty and again pulled her head erect as he cut her spinal cord in her neck and said, 'Good-bye, bitch.'"

Decker was pale with rage. His mind flashed to the department's mug shots of Betty Stevens. "Jetty, I appreciate your candor. If you can ever identify the doctors, let me know. The sheriff's department can deal in justice too!"

THE SHERIFF'S COVENANT

BILL DECKER, A student of criminal history, was sleeping fitfully. In his mind, he was determined to find a way to hit back at the cruel drug element in Dallas. The story of Betty Stevens's dastardly murder was the last damn straw. He was determined it would not go un-avenged.

His subconscious mind drifted to the saga of Tom Horn, who had been called in by the Wyoming Ranchers and Stock Growers Association; they were plagued by bands of roving rustlers. Tom Horn was paid as a vigilante to stalk rustlers in Wyoming. Horn was a deadly sniper killing the rustlers while they were in the act of stealing cattle and striking fear into the surviving gangs of cattle thieves. Then the words of Julius Caesar came into Decker's mind, "The best weapon against an enemy is another enemy."

It was about four o'clock in the morning when Decker sat straight up in bed and started laughing. A plan had taken shape in his mind. What he needed was a gang of cold-blooded mercenaries to deal with the dastardly drug element. He had just the man in mind to solve the Dallas drug problem.

September 1938, Benny Binion got a phone call from Bill Decker, Dallas County chief deputy in charge of criminal investigation. Decker was the real brains and energy behind the Dallas County sheriff's office. Smoot Schmid, the sheriff, was a likable but bumbling man who recognized Decker's talents and put him in charge of running things.

Decker told Binion in a phone call, "Benny, I want to see you right now, drop whatever you are doing and come to my office."

Benny was on the second floor of the old Southland Hotel counting the take from the previous night's run at the Southland's casino. "Are you goanna arrest me, Bill?"

"I don't know, come on over and we will talk about it." Both men laughed.

When Benny walked into the sheriff's office, Decker rose and came around his desk, put his hand on Benny's shoulder, and said, "Let's go up to the jail kitchen and get a cup of coffee. My office has eyes and ears and what I have to say is for your ears only!"

When they entered the jail kitchen on the fourth floor, Decker poured himself and Binion a cup of coffee and lit a Camel cigarette. Looking through the smoke, Decker said, "Benny, you are in a bunch of trouble."

This didn't bother Benny much as he had been in and out of trouble all his life. Decker continued, "As we speak, Joe Civello and his three sons are being arrested for dealing drugs." Benny was visibly shaken; Civello had been his close friend and confidant. Watching Benny's reaction, Decker asked, "Benny, you told me one time you would never have anything to do with dealing, are you still on the same page?"

"Decker, I don't want anything to do with the drugs or the pimps that handle that stuff."

"Fine, Benny, I got a proposition for you! Our Dallas crime

rate is roaring and at an all-time high. Dallas has the highest murder rate per capita in the United States. These damn Mafia drug dealers have created an unbearable crime wave. The users are desperate to get money for another fix. I know that a couple of your banks have been hit, and I'm sure the robberies are drug-related. You are the number one man on the street now. The Mafia will come to you to try to reestablish their drug business. I need your help to keep the Mafia and their drugs out of Dallas. I want you to put the word out on the street that the dealers are to leave town or else there is going to be a war, and either we run Dallas or the Mafia pill pushers will. They will send their hit squads but we will have an edge; I will know when they are coming! Get the locals before they get you. Be sure to dump the trash outside of Dallas County. I don't want the paperwork."

Decker watched Benny closely and took a long pull on his cigarette, and when Benny didn't object, Decker continued, "Make a list of your competitors in the gambling business here in Dallas and give it to your attorney and I'll give you a lock on Dallas County gambling. I'll run your competition out of town."

Benny's response came in rolls of laughter from deep inside, and wiping his eyes, he said, "Decker, that suits the hell out of me. I never liked those smart-head Diego bastards that come down here from Chicago anyway."

With this covenant, the door to the Dallas underworld slammed shut for the Mafia. A powerful Dallas mob boss had made a deal with a tough, smart Dallas lawman.

On several different occasions, Mafia hit men came to Dallas with a contract on Benny Binion, but on each occasion, with the help of Decker's female snitches in the horizontal trade, Decker was forewarned and intercepted the Chicago boys. What happened to those Chicago hit men is stranger than fiction. In each case, Decker took the guns away from the killers, put them in jail overnight, barefooted, and put them on the train to Chicago the next day without their shoes. Decker would wait a week or ten days and then mail their shoes back to them. The hit men were furious and complained that their constitutional rights had been violated. The FBI roared with laughter at the antics of the maverick Dallas lawman.

End Note

1.   Dr. Jack Hickman, who resides today in Dallas, was the county jail doctor and is the source for the story of Decker sending the Chicago hit men home without their shoes.

DALLAS VIGILANTES AT WORK, BODIES IN A DENTON COUNTY BARN

IT WAS JUST getting dark in downtown Dallas on Elm Street. The second-floor window of the Campbell Hotel slid open, and a Winchester Wildcat bolt action .22-caliber rifle with a four-power scope was placed gently on a small sandbag. The bullets for this deadly weapon were 30-06 cartridges necked down to accept a .22-caliber full metal jacket bullet.

A spotter watched through a pair of binoculars. He recognized the drug dealer as one of the hardcore dope peddlers that had failed to heed the warning that Binion had been put out on the streets of Dallas. The spotter spoke, "Mark your target, the man wearing a red silk shirt and a yellow straw hat. He is holding the drugs, I will count, and on the count of three, the money will have just changed hands."

An ex–Texas Ranger, a killer without his badge, was peering through the scope at a drug deal about to go down on a parking lot across the street. He had perfected a bullet that would not explode or expand when it found its mark; it would simply drill a small hole through its target.

The ranger had learned his lesson when he was detailed to investigate a serial killer's murders. The assassin was killing his victims in their sleep by driving an ice pick deep into the skull. There was no blood and it had been almost impossible to determine what the cause of death was.

The spotter counted. One, two, three. The money was now in the hands of the dealer. The gunman's finger tightened on the trigger and the bullet raced toward its target.

A metal tube at the muzzle of the rifle suppressed the impact of the sound to an almost silent splat and hid the muzzle flash.

It was the mission of the shooter to execute the drug dealers caught in the act. The full metal bullet made a clean kill. The projectile would penetrate the head of the victim, making only a small hole.

The drug dealer fell to the sidewalk—right in front of the startled customer. A white ambulance with a red cross painted on both sides appeared as if by magic and attendants dressed in white put the body on a gurney, which they lifted into the ambulance and shut the doors.

The ambulance drove out of sight before a crowd could gather. A few minutes later at the Gunther Macadam's funeral home on McKinney Avenue, the ambulance drivers rolled the body into the preparation room where it was injected with paraldehyde and rolled into a carpet. The rolled carpet was then placed in the back of a pickup truck and was en route to a barn just across the Denton County line not far from the city of Grapevine, Texas.

This scene was repeated time and time again at various locations in Dallas County. Fear finally overcame the greed of the Dallas drug dealers and they abandon the Dallas market. The ingenious plan of the Dallas sheriff with the help of Benny

Binion came to pass, and Dallas would stay drug-free until 1946 when Benny Binion was destined to leave Dallas.

Sheriff Decker's phone rang; it was W. F. Fry, the sheriff of Denton County. Sheriff Fry told Decker that eleven bodies had been found in a horse barn wrapped in rugs and wanted to know if he could send a deputy to Denton to help identify the bodies as he suspected they were Dallas criminal charters.

Decker dispatched Deputy Ed Castor and Hicky Bright to Denton to view the bodies. A phone call came in later that afternoon and Deputy Bright confirmed that all eleven of the bodies were Dallas drug dealers.

Decker called Benny Binion on the phone and asked him to dispose of the refuge in the horse barn. Benny responded that he understood and that the matter would be attended to.

Decker then called Sheriff Fry and told him that he would take care of the bodies and that the Denton sheriff's files could be closed. Two days later on a moonlit night, the eleven bodies along with two additional bodies were laid in a neat row on the road bed of a farm-to-market road that was being constructed just across the Dallas county line in Denton County. A large Caterpillar bulldozer driven by an ex–Texas Ranger belched black smoke as it pushed a mound of dirt over those Dallas drug dealers who have forever disappeared. We shall never know how many bodies are in that road bed, but fear overcame the drug dealers' greed and dealing in Dallas came to a halt.

THE MAFIA INVADES DALLAS

MEYER LANSKY, HEAD of the New York crime family, was impatient with Sam Giancana who had decided not to try to take over Dallas while Binion was boss. Dallas cash flow was just too tempting. Lansky sent Jack Nesbitt, a Kansas City don and cold-blooded hit man, to Dallas to reconnoiter.

Nesbitt found Hollis DeLois Green (his friends called him Lois) to be the perfect player. Nesbit came to Dallas, and while riding with Hollis Green on Commerce Street downtown Dallas. Green looked in his rearview mirror and saw his mark in the car behind them. Green slowed so the cars caught a red light. Green opened his car door, steps out, and puts a bullet in his mark's head. Jack Nesbit knew he had found the man for the Dallas action. Why use murder incorporated when a man like Green was available.

In March 1918, a son was born to Mary Addie Turner, a Tulsa Oklahoma prostitute. She gave the boy his father's last name, Green. They lived in a boarding house where Mary was not the only girl turning tricks there.

In 1930, Mary was badly beaten by a saloonkeeper who refused to pay her for her favors. Twelve-year-old Lois took offense and set out to even the score for his mother. He took a revolver that belonged to the proprietor of the boarding house and stalked the saloonkeeper. Lois made friends with the man's dogs, feeding them scraps.

Lois's opportunity came when the saloonkeeper's family left him at home alone while they went to church on Sunday. Lois climbed a tree only a few feet away from the bathroom window.

When the saloonkeeper came into the bathroom and sat on the toilet, Lois took careful aim and splattered the saloonkeeper's head all over the bathroom wall.

Lois climbed down from the tree, entered the house, and took all the disputed money from his victim's wallet and left.

Fearing that her son would be blamed for the saloonkeeper's murder, Mary moved to Dallas. Lois grew to be a big man, handsome, and over six feet tall, weighing over two hundred pounds. He mastered the art of fear and intimidation and often beat prostitutes he had working for him. On more than one occasion, girls would simply disappear.

The Dallas police department had a three-page arrest sheet on Green with only two convictions.

Then while burglarizing a Dallas pharmaceutical company, children playing hopscotch wrote down his license plate number on the sidewalk and later showed it to the police. At this point in his life, Sheriff Decker considered Lois as the prime suspect for twenty-two murders in Dallas.

Green was sent to Huntsville prison, where he sat at the knee of safecrackers, holdup men, burglars, and thieves. Lois listened to them explain their trade. He learned a valuable lesson when they told the mistake they made that got them caught.

When Lois got out of prison, he set up a safe house for ex-convicts. He made arrangements with a madam named Gladys

Harvey. Lois chose only the best ex-cons and invited them to his safe house. He gave them two hundred dollars, a new suit, and a girl of their choice. He would instruct them to wait for an assignment and took twenty-five percent off the top for setting up the deals. (When Harry McCormick of the *Times Herald* asked Green what his profession was, he answered, "I am a crime appraiser and identification consultant.")

His first Dallas hit, a cold windy winter day, Hollis DeLois Green, disguised as a street person, limps to the side of a car parked curbside. Two men sit in the car talking. Lois taps on the window and it is rolled down. Green empties a .45 into Ray Laudermilch and disappears around the corner of a building.

Lois moved ahead at a rapid pace. His gang was referred to as Green and the Forty Thieves and covered a broad spectrum of criminal activities, including murder for hire.

Jack Nesbitt, the Kansas City don, approached Lois Green with a list of Dallas gamblers. A five-thousand contract on each gambler and twenty thousand on Binion; in addition, Green was to receive twenty-five percent of the mob's Dallas gambling revenue once the purge was complete.

Jack Nesbitt told Lois to make it look like the Dallas gamblers were feuding among themselves to conceal the Mafia's invasion of Dallas. (Lansky and Nesbitt laughed behind closed doors as they planned a fatal accident for Green after he had eliminated the manifests of Dallas gamblers.)

Before each hit, the Green gang met and they held a drawing for Dallas gamblers that had not been eliminated.

THE CAR CHASE

THE NIGHT OF the car chase, Lois Green was driving and Pappy Drake, an excellent Dallas safecracker whose number had been drawn to hit a Dallas gambler, was riding shotgun. He chose the high-dollar mark Benny Binion.

The building that Binion was coming out of was the St. George Hotel on Commerce Street. It stood right across the street from the Adolphus Hotel.

As Binion's car pulls onto Pacific Street, a chase begins. Binion talks to his Mercury. (He has faith in his car.) Benny hits the main highway to his ranch in Grapevine, Texas, his Mercury quickly outdistancing the Cadillac. The Cadillac slowly closes the distance and they are roaring through the night, Binion's speedometer passing the one hundred mark as machine gun fire erupts from the pursuing car. Bullets are splattering into Binion's Mercury.

Binion brakes and swerves into the path of the Cadillac to prevent it from coming alongside. In retaliation, a burst of machine gun fire is fired into the rear of Binion's car that takes out the rear tires. Binion loses control of his Mercury and the dome light comes on as the car rolls and the driver side door comes open. Binion is thrown hard to the ground as the Mercury's door digs into the ground beside him. He sees the dome light come on as the car rolls over him. Binion's gun is lost in the crash as he lies stunned on the hard cold ground.

In the darkness, Binion staggers to his feet as the Cadillac makes a U-turn and stops beside the wreckage of his Mercury. Two men emerge from the Cadillac and rake Binion's car with machine gun fire as it ignites and explodes.

Binion realizes that he is not far from a neighbor's ranch house. Limping, he runs through the darkness. He sees that the lights of the ranch house are only a short distance away. His assailants chasing him, shouting his name, and cursing are firing at him into the darkness.

The ranch porch lights come on and the rancher comes to the porch cursing at the killers for firing so close to his house. The rancher fires an automatic rifle into the darkness toward Binion's tormentors. The ranch house dogs charge into the darkness; Benny crouches as the dogs run past him toward the men shouting and shooting.

This was more than the killers had bargained for. They couldn't pursuer any further against attacking dogs and the rancher's gunfire.

Binion hailed his neighbor from the front yard as the dogs, recognizing him, approached wagging their tails.

The two men went inside and the rancher opened a bottle of Scotch. Binion called his friend Sheriff Bill Decker, and Decker sent a squad car for him and a wrecker for the burned-up Mercury.

That same beautiful moonlit night, a sedan with three men were parked across the street from an elegant two-story home at 6808 Avalon one block north of the Lakewood Country Club on Gaston Avenue. One man remained behind the wheel while the other two men with shotguns move toward the house and hide in the bushes.

They had just reached their hiding places when the gang member at the wheel of the parked car flashed the lights three times, announcing the approach of Buddy Minyard's car, who was the operator of one of Binion's casinos.

Robert L. Minyard got out of his car to open the garage door, while his wife went to the side door of the house. The killers watched as the kitchen lights came on in the house and Minyard closed the garage door and started toward the rear door to the kitchen.

The two gunmen stepped from their hiding places, shotguns blazing. Minyard's body slumped to the ground. The gunmen scurried to their waiting car. Buddy's wife came from the kitchen to her fallen husband; he told her to call an ambulance as the killers' car drove into the darkness of the night. The Mafia invasion of Dallas was under way.

THE HANDWRITING ON THE WALL

I N 1946, BENNY Binion got a call from Meyer Lansky, head of
the New York crime family in charge of syndicated gambling
all across the United States.

Lansky told Benny, "We have just come out of a meeting
with a young senator from Tennessee, Estes Kefauver. He
has presidential aspirations—and has asked for the Mafia's
financial support and influence to get the Democratic
nomination. Estes is a standup guy. He told us right up front
that one of the planks in his platform would be an inquisition
into organized crime and gambling. We bargained with the
senator and asked that he use his influence to see that at least
one state would have legalized gambling. He agreed and told
us that Nevada, where gambling is already legal, would be left
that way." Lansky paused and then continued, "Benny, the Fed
is going to turn up the heat in all the major cities and close
down gambling. I don't know what you are going to do with this
information, but I am going to buy all the real estate I can get
in the two major cities in Nevada, Reno, and Las Vegas."

Benny did not have to be told twice. He put two million dollars in the trunk of a Cadillac automobile and drove to Las Vegas. When Benny Binion left Dallas for Las Vegas, the back door to the Dallas underworld swung open.

He purchased the El Dorado Club, put carpeting on the floor, and installed air-conditioning. He sent back to Erby Mayes in Dallas and bought cowboy uniforms for his dealers. He ordered Stetson hats from Resist All Hat Company in Garland, Texas, for all his employees.

Benny then changed the name of the casino to the Horseshoe Casino. He had a huge horseshoe made, painted it gold, and put it over the front door.

Benny used the same no-limit rules in Las Vegas that he had learned from Warren Diamond while managing the casino in the old Saint George Hotel on Commerce Street. His Horseshoe Casino was the only no-limit casino in the northern hemisphere and was taking in an average of $400 a minute, open twenty-four hours a day. That's where Benny got the money to buy a two-hundred-thousand-acre ranch in Montana from none other than Dallas oilman H. L. Hunt.

BINION LEAVES DALLAS

IT WAS LATE at night and the light was still on in Bill Decker's office. He rescued a file from the clutter of paper on his desk and studied it. A knock on the door startled him and he looked up. There stood Benny Binion, a grin on his face. Decker stood and said, "Come on in, Binion!"

Benny took a chair, spun it around, and straddled it, leaning his elbows on the chair, a cigar in his mouth. "Stopped in to say good-bye, Decker, I got a car waiting outside. I'm leaving for Las Vegas." Decker set the file aside and reached for a cigarette. "How long are you going to be gone, Benny?"

"It's gonna be a permanent move. As you know, the Fed is turning up the heat on gambling, so Johnny Merrill and I bought the El Dorado Club in Vegas. Bugsy Segal and his bunch are building a casino called the Flamingo that's going to be real flashy. Bugsy really liked what Fred Browning did at the Top O' Hill Casino in Arlington, and Bugsy had his architect spend some time at the Top O' Hill with Fred to draw up the plans for the Flamingo. We decided to just air-condition our casino and put some carpets on the floor and run our casino the same way Warren Diamond ran the St. George."

"You mean the no-limit betting?"

"Yeah, that's the main thing; we will be the only casino in the northern hemisphere that takes a no-limit bet. We figure that as the Fed closes gambling all across the states' business will really be good in Vegas."

Decker leaned back in his chair, looked at Binion, and said, "You're full of surprises, Benny. You've fought to keep the Dallas business for the last twenty-three years and now you are pulling up stakes. It won't be the same without you."

"I'm gonna miss Dallas, Decker, but it's a matter of economics. It's costing me over a million dollars a year to meet all the fines and payola to keep my casinos open here." Decker whistled softly and Benny continued. "I can buy any casino in Vegas for what it takes to make one month's payola payments here in Dallas."

Decker had a mischievous grin on his face as he asked, "The pending warrant for operating a policy wheel wouldn't have anything to do with your decision to leave town, would it?"

Benny leaned forward and relit his cigar. "The politicians get their usual handout. We've had the same district attorney for the last ten years. Now all of a sudden, the DA gets a bad case of the 'do-rights' and wants to nail me instead of looking the other way, I don't know what his problem is. I'm just glad they're telegraphing their punch. You tell me what's going on, Decker?"

Taking a deep pull on his cigarette making the end glow, Decker slowly exhaled and said, "I'll tell you what I think. I think someone is putting the pressure on the DA and I think it's coming from out of town, like Chicago."

Benny chewed his cigar as he spoke. "Now it's your turn to watch your back, Decker. I honestly don't know who or what element is going to take over my business. When the boys asked me about my Dallas plans, I told 'em the party is over in Dallas."

Decker interrupted Benny. "Benny, you are smart. I can't tell you how glad I am that you're not going to try to hold the Dallas operation together. My friends with the FBI tell me that there is a sting operation incubating that is going to put politicians that are taking payola on the spot."

Benny shifted in his chair. "Call it a gambler's hunch, but I think the policy wheel thing is just the tip of the iceberg, and if I can't win, I ain't gonna play. Anyway I'm leaving Dallas and I told the boys it's every man for himself."

"Benny, I appreciate what you have done for Dallas, helping me keep the drugs off the streets."

Benny laughed. "I sure got a kick out of the way you kept sending the Chicago boys back to the Windy City without their shoes. Decker, I gotta tell you about what I call my Washburn file; I been paying the mayor sixty thousand a year and each city councilman twenty thousand a year to look the other way. Councilman Washburn calls me and asks me, 'Where's my twenty thousand, Binion? I haven't received it yet!'"

Benny laughed as he recalled that he assured the councilman he had already been paid. At that point, the councilman became belligerent and shouted, "It doesn't matter, it's gonna take another twenty thousand to keep me in line!"

Laughing, Benny said, "I didn't argue further with him. I told him I would have Vido deliver the money to him. I hung up the phone and hollered for Vido and told him to get two hundred of those counterfeit hundred-dollar bills we got off that Chicago drug dealer, put them in a grocery sack, and take them to Councilman Washburn."

Both men were roaring with laughter, and Benny, catching his breath, asked Decker to let him know if Councilman Washburn's wife got caught passing queer money at the grocery store. "What's Washburn gonna tell the DA, 'That's money I got from Benny Binion as a bribe'?"

Sobering up, Benny said, "I gotta leave now, Decker, and I'm gonna ask a favor. My father, Lonnie, is in poor health and we put him in the Gaston Avenue Sanitarium. Would you check in on him occasionally?"

As Benny left Decker's office, the two men shook hands. Benny said, "You should run for sheriff, Decker. You've been running this place for the last fifteen years anyway. If you do run and I hope you do let me know, I will help you get elected."

Decker later learned that one of the sanitarium's patients had died penniless, with no family, and no one came to claim the body. Benny called a friend in the undertaking business and asked him to bury the sanitarium's patient as nice as he knew how and to send him the bill.

BEN WHITAKER'S RANCH
AT GARLAND, TEXAS

THE ORREN W. Whitaker family name appears in the 1910 Dallas census indexes with a Beckley Street address in Oak Cliff. Benjamin F. Whitaker is the fourth child born. He will be later known as Ben F. Whitaker and would, in Benny Binion's words, *have Dallas.*

> Johnny Scott, whose family owned and ran Scott's Sandwich Stand where the local high school students hung out, remembered Ben Whitaker. "He got his hair cut at Green's Barbershop down on the old Garland square. He always wore cowboy boots and drove a Lincoln Zephyr."

Will Fritz got a phone call from Ben Whitaker. "Your presence at my BBQ Saturday would add luster to the affair. Several of your friends will be there. Be sure and bring your

Thompson with you." Will agreed to attend the BBQ, which was held at Whitaker's ranch in Garland.

Dallas County Sheriff Smoot Smith and Chief Deputy Bill Decker were among the guests. While the ranch cadre put the finishing touches on the BBQ being prepared lakeside, Whitaker took the group on a tour of his horse stables, the exercise track, and a nine-hole golf course that he had laid out behind his two-story white-framed ranch house.

As the group toured the ranch, Whitaker explained, "The ranch was originally an eight-hundred-acre tract of land owned by W. R. 'Will' Kingsley who liked to be referred to as Colonel Kingsley.

"He always wore a white suit and a wide-brimmed white hat. Originally, the ranch had a wagon trail running through it that would later be named Kingsley Road after Colonel Kingsley.

"Colonel Kingsley had purchased the land to raise cotton. When the cotton market got soft, he sold the south half of the ranch to Randolph Caldwell. The part we're on now is what Mr. Caldwell purchased."

> Joseph Caldwell, Randolph Caldwell's surviving son, 3621 Cornell Drive, Dallas, Texas, reflected, "Back in the '30s, Dad sold or traded one-half of the ranch on the south side of Kingsley Road to a fellow named Ted Monroe, a Dallas criminal attorney. There was a beautiful white house on the crown of a wooded hill overlooking a man-made lake and a large red horse barn. Monroe later sold the property to Ben Whitaker, who kept a lot of his racehorses there. I remember meeting Whitaker one time when I was a little kid. He talked about putting his horses in all the important races, but I don't remember much about him other than that."

Ben Whitaker continued, "Now the reason I've asked Will Fritz and Bill Decker to bring their machine guns is because I have an old stump that's in the way of an exercise track that I'm building for my horses. I thought it would add luster to our party if the two lawmen would dig the stump out with their machine guns." Decker and Fritz stood toe to toe, the muzzles of their machine guns pointed at the old tree stump.

What Whitaker hadn't told Decker or Fritz was that Deputy Bill Wiseman, the demolition expert for the Dallas County sheriff's department, had put a half-pint whiskey bottle with some nitroglycerin at the base of the stump. A cheer went up as the stump was destroyed with a loud bang. The BBQ was served and the politicians began their politicking.

BLACK CLOUDS GATHERING

IT WAS IN May 1947 that lightning struck Benny's policy wheels and horse parlors. It was the end of an era that was brought about by the Kefauver senatorial inquisition into organized crime and gambling. A warrant went out for Binion's arrest for illegal gambling. But Benny had headed Meyer Lansky's warning and had left Dallas for Las Vegas in 1946. He had purchased the El Dorado Casino in Vegas. While Bugsy Segal floundered with the mob's money building the Flamingo Hotel and Casino, Benny went into fast-forward with both boots on the ground.

Once again, Benny's casino was the only place in the northern hemisphere where you could get a no-limit bet. His Diamond Horseshoe Casino was taking in $400 a minute, open twenty-four hours a day. He worked the same no-limit format in Las Vegas he had learned from Warren Diamond in Dallas. He put the Vegas police department in his pocket. He always obliged the Vegas police department with loan of money for their narcotics stings.

Binion became king of the hill in Las Vegas as Bugsy Segal's Flamingo Casino floundered with construction overruns and the Mafia mob smoldered with resentment.

Because it was common knowledge federal agents monitored the casino phone lines, a delegation called on Benny in person at his Horseshoe Casino. He recognized the casino owners, but not the Mexican nationalist who accompanied them. They asked for a private meeting and were ushered to a room above the casino. The spokesman for the group proposed a plan to launder money by mingling it with the cash flow of the Horseshoe, a nice commission to be negotiated.

The moment Benny saw the well-dressed nationalist with their dark sunglasses, he knew it was drug money they wanted to launder. Benny explained that while he was not averse to making more money, a man could eat only so much steak and drink only so much beer.

Bullets riddled his car and ignition bombs were dismantled as frequently as they were attached. Binion had been through the drill. He had too many people on his payroll to be caught off guard. But the mob conspired and decided that the best way to get rid of Binion was the same way they got rid of Capone in Chicago. Tip off the Fed to do an IRS audit on the old policy wheel business in Dallas.

Binion's Dallas partner and bookkeeper Harry Urban was surprised when FBI agents entered his office with a warrant to take Binion's books and records. Benny's arrest and detainment in the Dallas County jail ensued in 1953.

Sheriff's Deputy Lieutenant Bill Wiseman always went to work early so he could stop by the Dallas prison inmate John Arnolds's jailhouse shoe-shine stand before checking in for duty. Benny Binion had his boots shined every morning, sometimes getting to John's stand before Lieutenant Wiseman. Bill admired the beautiful boots worn by Benny and asked one morning, "Mr. Binion, may I ask you a personal question?"

Benny replied, "You bet, son. I may not answer you, but you may ask. I consider us friends!"

Bill Wiseman asked, "How much did those boots cost?"

Binion hollered, "Way too much, sinful! Ieeeeeee!"

Both men laughed and Lieutenant Wiseman never did learn how much Binion's boots had cost him.

Benny's trial didn't go very well. He had to pay $862,538.47 in back taxes and another $20,000 in fines. It seems there was some confusion about the proceeds paid to the policy wheel winners. It was Benny's understanding that the wheels returned eighty percent of the premium income back to the players.

When the IRS accounts audited the books, it turned out the players were getting twenty percent and the wheels were retaining eighty percent.

Benny stood with his attorney Murray Hughes facing U.S. District Judge Ben Rice. He peeled off $20,000 from his pocket to pay his fine. He had another $100,000 in his pocket to pay the judge for a suspended sentence, but the FBI intervened and thwarted the attempted bribe.

HERBERT "THE CAT" NOBLE

MAUDE SANTERRE NOBLE gave birth to her first son, April 21, 1909. He was named Herbert, after his father. Fifty-five years earlier, Maude's parents had left France where the Santerre name was well respected. The Santerres were considered activists and were among the principal zealots that started the French Revolution years earlier. They had served as constabulary and guarded the aristocratic French prisoners as they were driven through the streets of Paris to the guillotine. Legend has it that a family member actually pulled the lanyard that dropped the blade, which beheaded Marie Antoinette.

The Industrial Revolution had brought unemployment, and the Santerre family was unable to find work. They joined a French socialist colony named La Reunion that sailed for Galveston, Texas, in 1854. The ill-fated colony was on its way to what they envisioned as fertile land along the banks of the Trinity River, which they had purchased from a French land agent. Spirits were high as they viewed their newly acquired property in the spring months of their arrival.

The La Reunion colonist planted vineyards with their precious grapevine cuttings brought from France. They were enthusiastic, only to have their hopes dashed when, in the latter part of August, there were twenty-one days of temperatures exceeding one hundred degrees and no rain for almost two months. The vines withered and died; the venture had failed.

Most of the colonists were not farmers by trade and walked away in despair. The Santerre family, determined to make a stand, stayed with their land and purchased additional parcels of land from the departing colonists.

It would seem, however, that a curse followed the Santerre family as, one by one, they were struck down with tuberculosis.

We know today that infected cows pass the disease on to humans through their milk. Even though their dairy herd was infected, Maude Santerre was fortunate to survive the curse, and her son, Herbert Noble, would rise from poverty and despair to be, in his day, a West Dallas legend.

As a young boy, Herbert worked in his father's business and was exposed to grown men and their games of dice and cards played during the lunch hour. Almost all men at that time in our history were afflicted with gambling fever as it was almost impossible to earn enough to survive working for wages. Gambling was their only hope if only to get ahead for a short time.

Herbert had a quick mind and realized the opportunity for an astute gambler. His father, aware of his son's interest in gambling, told him to leave it alone or become a professional. Still in his teens, Herbert decided to become a professional. The young boy learned all the tricks, how to mark cards, deal from the bottom, deal seconds, and how to cook dice so they either would or would not come up with a seven.

He observed the violence of the games of chance and

decided to carry a gun so he would have an edge in the event of confrontation. Herbert had no intention of letting some dim-witted thug beat him senseless.

With his newfound courage carrying a gun, he expanded his territory. Herbert became what was called a bush gambler. He had found there was a much better chance of winning if he stayed away from downtown Dallas and gambled with the not-so-savvy small-town gamblers.

It was at the conclusion of a dice game at the Red Bird Airport that Herbert decided to use some of his newly acquired money to take flying lessons from Jessie Akins, an instructor, using a J-3 Piper airplane to respond to another of his boyhood passions, flying.

In 1938, Noble, then twenty-nine, took a job working with Sam Murray's gang in Dallas as a bodyguard along with some other West Dallas toughs, Tommy Yates and Jimmy Wilson. Sam Murray was an intruder operating outside the jurisdiction of the Dallas gambling syndicate. He wasn't paying his dues.

The operation of Murray's organization was intruding on Ivy Miller's turf, one of Binion's lieutenants. Tuesday morning, June 19, 1940 at 10:30 a.m. in front of the Dallas National Bank building at 1500 Commerce Street, witness saw Sam Murray waiting for the streetlight to turn; he was telling Jimmy Wilson a joke. As the two men crossed Commerce Street to enter the bank, Ivy Miller stepped from the bank door and emptied a .38 Colt automatic into Sam Murray. Sam made a play for his pistol but was too late. Murray's last words as he crumbled to the street in front of at least twenty witnesses were, "Miller, you rat bastard!"

Jimmy Wilson faded into the crowd as policemen from a passing police car apprehended Ivy Miller. Miller later pleaded self-defense and was no billed.

Herbert Noble was smart enough to realize he had aligned himself with the wrong team and approached Binion with an olive branch in hand. Binion found Noble likable and intelligent.

He granted Noble permission to operate in Dallas as long as he paid the syndicate twenty-five percent off the top.

Noble was energetic and worked smart. He asked for and got permission to open a casino of his own, the Airman's Club located at the intersection of Ervay and Pacific downtown Dallas.

Ray Laudermilk, who had first worked for Binion as a street man, steering customers to Binion's dice tables, had worked his way up to be one of Binion's policy wheel bosses. He approached Noble with a plan to open a new policy wheel without Binion or the syndicate's permission. The always-ambitious Herbert Noble had strayed again as he went into the policy wheel venture with Laudermilk.

When Noble learned that Ray Laudermilk was found full of bullet holes dead in the backseat of his Cadillac sedan, he immediately found Binion and put himself in the best light possible and asked to be and was forgiven for stepping out of bounds.

In the meantime, Noble had won some oil leases in a dice game, which turned out to be very profitable. He used this money along with his gambling income to purchase some rural acreage in Denton County west of Lewisville and not far from Grapevine, Texas. A landing strip and a hangar were constructed on Noble's newly acquired land and he bought three airplanes, an L-19 Cessna, a Stearman biplane, and a Beechcraft Staggerwing. He built overnight accommodations for high-dollar poker games and intended to build a grand casino comparable to Fred Browning's Top O' Hill Casino.

In 1945, Las Vegas was nothing but a dusty crossroad as you crossed the Nevada desert on the way to and from Los Angeles. Bugsy Segal, Mafia don and boyhood friend of Sam Giancana, Chicago Mafia chieftain, stopped to eat at the only restaurant in Las Vegas; when he sat down, he heard the drone of a croupier's voice as he called out the action on the dice table in the next room. Bugsy thought to himself, "That guy has a great voice."

He made small talk with the waitress and learned that gambling was legal in Las Vegas. World War II was winding down, Germany had just fallen, and it would be only a matter of time before Japan would surrender. Bugsy envisioned returning GIs, their pockets bulging with mustering out pay, stopping in Las Vegas for a little fun. He thought of Fred Browning's Top O' Hill Casino in Arlington, Texas, and decided to convince his Mafia friends to build a casino just like Fred's right here in Las Vegas.

Binion, back in Dallas, gave full disclosure about his move to Las Vegas. Noble was given the opportunity to go along; he, however, decided that this was his opportunity to take over the Dallas action.

In December of 1946, when Benny left Dallas for Las Vegas, the back door to the Dallas underworld swung open. Sam Giancana, the Chicago Mafia chieftain, sent Paul Roland Jones and Jack Nappi, two Mafia chieftains, to Dallas to bribe the newly elected sheriff Steve Guthrie. The deal was $150,000 up front and $4,000 a month with the mob's guarantee that he could be sheriff for as long as he wanted. In exchange, all Guthrie had to do was look the other way when it came to prostitution, drugs, and gambling in Dallas, Texas.

Unfortunately for the two Mafia liaisons, the newly elected sheriff Steve Guthrie, who was an ex–Dallas city policeman and World War II veteran, turned the tables on them when he had the meetings bugged. Mafioso dons Jack Nappi and Paul Roland Jones were convicted and put in jail.

Sam Giancana, the Chicago Mafia chieftain, waited until May 1947 to make his second attempt to take control of the Dallas underworld. He sent a member of Chigaco's Jewish Mafia family Me Chiai to Dallas, Jack Ruby. Giancana's instructions for Ruby were to give Hollis DeLois Green, a deadly and sadistic Dallas hit man, contracts on all high-profile Dallas gamblers.

Ruby told Green to create an atmosphere of deceit portraying an intermural civil war between local Dallas gamblers and their struggle for control of the Dallas underworld's cash flow.

Giancana advised Ruby to bypass the hard-nosed sheriff's department and establish a beachhead for Mafia operations by purchasing Dallas taverns and honky-tonks, which would be transformed into erotic strip joints and distribution points for prostitution, narcotics, and gambling.

Ruby's first acquisition was the Silver Spur Club, then the Sovereign Club, next the Vegas Club on Oak Lawn. A short time later, he purchased Bob Welk's ranch house, a downtown Dallas honky-tonk. Then he bought the Carousel Club across Commerce Street from the prestigious Adolphus Hotel where the St. George Hotel once stood.

Like rising floodwater from the Trinity River, the Mafia operations engulfed Dallas. Their business was so good that they built their own bank to launder their drug and gambling money, the Merchant's State Bank on Ross Avenue.

With Binion out of the way, the ambitious Herbert Noble was the priority target for Dallas's number one hit man Hollis DeLois Green and his gang of forty thieves. There was a ten-thousand-dollar contract on Noble's life. The gang met at Sky View, a nightclub on Fort Worth Avenue and had drawings to see who got the contract on Noble.

The first attempt was made in January 1946. You might say just as Binion drove out of sight. A whisper was put on the street for Noble to hear that Binion was still mob boss in Dallas and it was Binion that ordered the hit on Noble. The second attempt came late at night in May 1948. Noble drove through the gate to his ranch and a waiting gunman riddled his car with machine gun fire. Noble took a slug in his left arm. He used his tie as a tourniquet to stem the flow of blood from his arm and gave chase.

Under the cover of darkness on November 10, 1948, one of Green's men who had won the night's raffle to hit Noble hid in a duck blind on a lake that was overlooked by Noble's ranch house. The sniper waited with a thermos of coffee and a high-powered rifle with a nine-power scope. He took his shot and missed, then ran as Noble came from his ranch house firing a .30-caliber carbine. Noble retrieved a thermos half full of coffee from the duck blind.

Still another attempt was made on Valentine's Day 1949. Noble spotted a dynamite bomb before he turned on the car's ignition. The following September, Noble spotted Jack Nesbitt, one of Green's accomplice, through binoculars as Nesbitt drove up the ranch road. Noble shouted and told Todd Ellis, his ranch foreman, to bring the car around. Noble raced into the house and emerged with his favorite weapon, an M1 carbine. A car chase ensued and Noble shot out the tires on Nesbitt's car causing it to crash.

Noble and his foreman circled back to the crashed vehicle. The occupants had emerged and splattered Noble's car with machine gun fire. Once back at the ranch, Noble noticed blood had soaked his shoe, a bullet was lodged in his left leg. He called his friend Bill Decker, and Decker sent an ambulance with a deputy to escort Noble to the Dallas Methodist Hospital.

Decker showed up shortly after Noble was admitted. Harry McCormick with the *Dallas Times Herald* entered hospital room. After Noble described the shooting, Decker asked, "Do you know who your assailants were?"

Noble replied, "Sure I know who they were, I got a good look at them through my binoculars!"

Noble, however, refused to divulge any names. Harry McCormick asked, "Isn't this the ninth time they've tried to kill you?"

Noble counted on his fingers and replied, "Yeah, that's right, nine times!"

Bill Decker laughed and said, "Herbert 'the Cat' Noble!"

Headlines in the *Dallas Times Herald* the next day read, HERBERT 'THE CAT' NOBLE CHEATS DEATH AGAIN

Decker knew that Noble had plans of his own and was not surprised when Green managed to get another shot at Noble before he left the hospital. Janice Denton, a night nurse for Noble, recalled that a couple of days after Noble was admitted, she heard gunfire and then car tires squealed as the lights in Noble's room went out. She rushed into Noble's room to find him on the floor with a pistol in his hand.

It was only a few days later when Nelson Harris, a high-profile Dallas gambler, and his pregnant wife were killed. Five sticks of dynamite attached to the top of his car's transmission exploded when the ignition was switched on.

Jack Ruby passed along another name to be added to Lois Green's hit list. Louis Tindrell, gambler in charge of the Tarrant County action in Fort Worth, was ambushed when he and his wife returned from the theater to their home.

The Green gang also made two unsuccessful attempts to hit Benny Binion. One was a failed sniper's attack on Benny as his Cadillac spread north toward Sherman on Highway 75. The other attempt was dynamite attached to his Cadillac ignition. Always cautious, Benny spotted the bomb before the car was started.

Noble and some partners had plans to purchase Hicks airfield in Fort Worth. A meeting was scheduled for a breakfast meeting at T. J. Gracias's to firm up their offer and write a letter of intent. Ordinarily he would drive his souped-up Mercury. He told his wife, Mildred, that he wanted to use her Cadillac. It would make a better impression.

On November 5, 1949, Mildred Noble, age thirty-six, got behind the wheel of her husband's car and turned the key in the ignition. There was a blinding flash and loud explosion as a nitroglycerin bomb exploded. Car parts rained down on the neighborhood, and Mildred's burned, faceless body was hurled into the street, where it lay smoldering.

Herbert Noble was crazed with grief and sat for days staring at his wife's picture. Weeks later, when he finally emerged from morning, he visited Bill Decker. Decker opened the file on Mildred Noble's death. After reviewing the file, Noble said, "It doesn't make any difference. I know who is responsible!" When Noble left Decker's office, he noticed that Noble walked with a limp.

Herbert Noble's mind was tormented with grief and rage. Seeking revenge for his wife's death, he prepared a list of the Green gang's members who had knowledge of explosives. Number one on the list was Jack Todd, who was nicknamed "Dynamite Jack Todd." It was Noble's intent to systematically destroy those members and Benny Binion, as Jack Ruby had told Noble that Binion was working with Lois Green to get rid of him.

Noble's first mission was to abduct Jack Todd and take him on a one-way ride. He held a cocked .45 automatic pistol pointed at Todd's head as he drove down Singleton past Fish Trap Road in West Dallas.

Todd realized he was a dead man and used combat knowledge he had learned in the Marine Corps. Jamming his hand over the muzzle of the .45 automatic held by Noble, Todd knew that forced the firing mechanism into a locked-safe position. Todd lunged at Noble and bit off a part of his ear. He kicked the passenger's side door open and rolled out onto the pavement. Two sheriff's deputy squad cars were parked nearby. The deputies in conference were surprised to see the consternation in the street and turned on their red lights and siren coming to Todd's rescue. Todd, however, true to his gangland code would not press charges against Noble who was taken to Parkland Hospital to have his ear repaired.

One o'clock Saturday morning, December 24, 1949, a still-unsolved murder was committed when a man, his face covered with a ski mask, stepped from the darkness of the parking lot of the Sky View Nightclub and empties a shotgun into Lois Green at point-blank range.

Hearing the shots, Jack Todd, Green's best friend and trusted lieutenant, rushed from the club. Jack knelt beside Green, then turned to the gathering crowd and shouted, "Someone call an ambulance!" Louis Green recognized Jack but was unable to speak.

A witness told sheriff's deputies that the shooter limped away and simply disappeared into the darkness. Binion realized how dangerous Noble had become and sent Harold Shimley, a smooth-talking con man who could charm the birds right out of the trees, to see Noble.

Shimley had been in the oil business in Oklahoma, got his hands on some money, and came to Las Vegas to double it. Instead, he lost it all and tried to commit suicide. Benny heard the story and gave Shimley a job to get him back on his feet. Shimley's mission for Benny was to set up a telephone conference and be in the same room with Noble when the telephone call went down. Binion wanted to convince Noble that he was not the rascal Jack Ruby said he was, that he considered him a friend and certainly meant him no harm. The meeting was set and the phone conference went as planned but Noble didn't buy it.

On August 7, 1951, at 11:00 a.m., Green gang members Jim Thomas and Jack Nesbitt were hidden behind bushes a little over one hundred yards from Herbert Noble's mailbox just outside a cattle guard on the ranch road leading to the ranch house. Jim Thomas watched through binoculars as Noble's car approached his mailbox. Thomas said, "Now!" and Jack Nesbitt touched a ground wire on the Gulf automobile battery to the barbwire fence in the bushes where they hid and a nitroglycerin bomb buried under the cattle guard exploded. The explosion stunned the two killers but they scrambled to their blue 1950 pickup truck and sped away.

Herbert Noble's car was demolished and nothing was found

of him but the tip of his thumb. The ace of spades from a poker deck survived the blast and fluttered down onto the smoking debris. That was the thirteenth and final attempt on Noble's life. The postman who had just made his run told Sheriff Decker, "There was no mail put in the box that day."

The reported number of deaths in the Dallas gang wars had reached forty-seven. The actual number will never be known. Herbert "the Cat" Noble, the West Dallas gambler who had risen from the defeat and despair of an ancestry plagued with bad luck, had hit the end of his chain, but he left an indelible mark in the annals of Dallas history.

A posh residential development named Noble's Point stands today where Herbert Noble had plans for his grand casino to rival Fred Browning's Top O' Hill Casino in Arlington, Texas.

THE SLEEP OUT

08/16/04 **James Virgil Counts** 6935 E. 15 #125
Tulsa, Oklahoma 7412-7406

Born May 12, 1921, in Henrietta, Oklahoma, Virg was first incarcerated at the age of thirteen in Gatesville, Texas, reformatory. He spent twenty-seven years of his life in prison behind bars.

Known in the trade as a knob knocker, Mr. Counts was a safecracker. While in Leavenworth, he met Benny Binion. The Texas and Oklahoma boys sort of hung together and were well liked by the prison guards because they did their jobs without whining.

When Benny arrived at Leavenworth, his former Dallas partner Harry Urban already had a job making shoes. Benny got a job with the prison fire department as chief monitor. The prison would have been hard to burn. It was solid concrete. Everyone liked Benny. He was tough-minded, but had a great sense of humor and was fun to be around.

Benny was incarcerated with the likes of "Machine Gun"

Kelly and Harvey Bailey, both suspects in the Kansas City massacre.

Benny and Virg got to be good friends and managed to get a job "sleeping out," meaning they spent the night outside the walls. One of their details was, they, along with three other inmates, were assigned to a work detail in the prison dairy barn.

The men milked the cows in the morning, then again in the evening. The dairy foreman, a state employee, enjoyed a bottle on occasion. Sometimes he would fall asleep after his evening toddy.

The five prison dairymen had been trading milk for beer with a Choctaw Indian woman, whose family owned the Midnight Sun, a honky-tonk located a little less than a mile from the prison dairy.

One night while watching their foreman consume an unusual amount of the whiskey, they decided to make a trip to the Midnight Sun. As luck would have it, they came away clean and with some new friends outside the walls.

The inmates continued to visit the Midnight Sun. What had been good-natured rivalry between the inmates and the Indians one night got a little too rambunctious and a fight broke out.

The local sheriff was called and the inmates were taken to the county jail. When asked to produce identification, they had none and suggested that it was probably lost on the parking lot where the skirmish had taken place.

The sheriff, unconvinced, sent a deputy to search for the lost wallets. When the deputy returned empty-handed, the sheriff became suspicious and contacted the prison wardens' office. This was all taking place in the wee hours of the morning before the prison's normal head count.

Much to the embarrassment of the dairy foreman, he was unable to account for the missing prisoners who worked at the dairy.

The sheriff returned the inmates to the prison authorities. The incident was the only blemish on Benny's prison record; he was released early in 1957 for time off for good behavior.

One of the best friends Benny made while he was in prison was the prison chaplain. Benny told the chaplain he was a gambler by trade and he bet there was a heaven. He explained further that if he was right, he would win a place in heaven. He would try to lead a good life so he could get in. Laughing, Benny said, "If it's not a good bet, it doesn't make any difference anyway." The Catholic chaplain found Benny's outlook on religion a challenge and encouraged him to attend confirmation classes. Benny did attend and embraced the Catholic religion. When he was released on parole in 1957, he was a confirmed Catholic.

THE LOW POINT IN
BENNY'S CAREER

WHEN THE PRISON gates at Leavenworth swung open for Benny, he was fifty-two years old. He had done forty-two months of hard time. Eddie Levinson, a silent partner, ran the Horseshoe while Benny had been, as they say, "out of town."

Part of the casino's profits had been skimmed to pay Lansky, the Mafia don in charge of all syndicated gambling. That plus having paid almost a million dollars in back taxes and obscene attorney's fees, Benny wasn't broke but he was badly bent. Looking back at that time in his history, it was a definite low. Benny mentally gritted his teeth and took hold of his bootstraps and said to himself, "Here we go again!"

Benny called on an old friend in Dallas, Troy Post, chairman of the board of The Great Americana Corporation, which controlled Gulf Life and American Life Insurance companies. Benny told Troy that the Horseshoe needed a face-lift and he needed a loan.

One of the first things Benny did with the fresh capital was to encase a seven-foot horseshoe on the front of the casino and paint it gold. He asked for bids for carpeting and air-conditioning.

The state of Nevada was anxious to keep him and he was eager to remain. Benny was a driving engine and they appreciated him. His message was, this is a casino for serious gamblers, no holds barred. Benny's crap tables offered a $500 limit, ten times the maximum at other casinos. His loose slots paid the best odds in town. People came directly from work without even changing clothes to play the wall-to-wall slots. The new limits made the Horseshoe famous. Benny put out the word—the Horseshoe is where the action is.

In November 1980, a fellow by the name of William Lee Bergstrom, from Austin, Texas, asked Benny if he could bet a million dollars at the dice table.

Benny paused and said, "As long as you bet it all on the first roll."

Bergstrom's next question was, "May I put it anywhere on the tale?"

To which Benny replied, "Yes!"

Bergstrom's entourage approached a table where a game was in progress. As the dice were passed to a new shooter, Bergstrom chose to place the money on the "don't pass" line. He laid the black suitcase on the back line. The new shooter was a fine-looking lady who severed out in three rolls. The croupier announced a back line winner and looked at Bergstrom. He let out a fierce rebel yell and pounded the table and yelled, "Yes! Yes! Yes!" He and his two suitcases filled with money were escorted to a waiting car.

The next year, Bergstrom brought another suitcase filled with a million dollars and placed it on the "don't pass" line; the dice came out on the first roll a six and an ace. When the seven turned up on the first roll, Bergstrom looked like he had been struck by a bolt of lightning. He left the Horseshoe never to return.

THE PRINCE OF TOUCH

Benny, like his friend back in Dallas, Sheriff Bill Decker, kept a very informal office. He did business from a booth in the downstairs restaurant of the Horseshoe Casino. Nobody needed an appointment to talk with Benny. They could just howdy with him, shake hands, and be invited to join him for a bowl of chili. Many a gnarled, old, bowlegged rodeo rider will tell you Benny Binion saved rodeo when he brought the national finals to Las Vegas. Benny saw the rodeo business floundering and used his money and influence to move the action from Oklahoma to Las Vegas.

Benny was always ready to help a cowboy down on his luck. He often loaned the necessary money for rodeo contestants' entrance fees. Money for feed bills, veterinarian's bills, and more often than not, paid hospital bills for his cowboy friends with broken bones. Benny would often sweeten the pot when he considered it short to make the rider's efforts more worthwhile. He was always a buyer if a rodeo rider was in a pinch and needed to sell his horse. He would pay the top dollar for the distressed sale.Benny didn't wallow in his millions. He liked to quote his oil rich friend, Sid Richardson, a Texas millionaire, who said, "Money has no home, anybody can go broke, anybody!" Sid told Benny he was happier when he was hustling, trying to put together a wildcat oil field, than he was with the billion dollars he was sitting on.

Benny remained a Texas tough guy. He didn't shave every day. He defiantly carried a pistol, which was against the rules for an ex-con, and he was never far from his favorite weapon a twelve-gauge sawed-off pump shotgun.

The Horseshoe Casino was Benny's "cash cow." He always savored that time of day when he would call the casino's bank and ask, "What was our take today?" The Horseshoe was the only place in the world you could bet a million on one turn of the cards or on one roll of the dice; lose your car, your truck, or your wife's diamond ring, and if you won, Benny would offer to flip a coin double or nothing.

At age eighty-four, Benny, the multimillionaire gambler and horse trader, was living in a spacious house trailer located on his two-hundred-thousand-acre ranch in Montana. He had purchased the ranch from none other than H. L. Hunt in Dallas. His main passion was trading horses. Showing horseflesh to Benny Binion was like showing a hooker your bank roll. He bred and raised thousands of horses. He didn't pay much attention to bloodlines. He said, "I always just looked at the individual horse, 'cause a lot of times, a good horse will have a dink for a brother."

Giving his hat a tug, Benny said, "I don't raise race horses, but if Texas goes back to pari-mutuel, I've got my eye on a piece of ground down there, and I may just start raising thoroughbreds."

SHERIFF DECKER'S FUNERAL
AND BENNY'S PROPERTY
ON INWOOD LANE

H E HAD BEEN sheriff of Dallas County for twenty-one years. He was so popular that no one ever filed to run against him. Twice he was asked to run for the U.S. Senate and twice he said, "The sheriff's office is in such a mess no one can straighten it out but me, I better just stay a sheriff."

Many of his deputies had a father fixation on Decker. There was indeed enough difference in age to justify this relationship. He had certainly scolded and praised them as if they were his children. In addition to this, there was the bond of comrade-in-arms, the esprit de corps born of sharing a place in harm's way and knowing that you can count on your comrades to protect your back.

While he was convalescing at home, the deputies would take turns sitting with him. One of the newer deputies that was mortally afraid of Sheriff Decker had refused to take his turn to sit with him. A. D. McCurley, a veteran deputy who was somewhat mischievous, took the younger deputy aside. He told him that Decker had just been given a new drug that would allow him to sleep peacefully through the night.

The veteran assured him there would be no problem. He further instructed the apprehensive deputy to show up at the appointed time, check on Decker, and then help himself to some food in the icebox. He should then turn on the TV and make himself comfortable for the rest of his watch.

Following the instructions of his cohort, the young deputy settled into Decker's favorite chair, adjusting the TV to his favorite program—Monday night football. After a couple of trips to the icebox and the conclusion of the football game, the deputy nodded off.

It was almost 3:00 a.m. when Decker noticed the light was on in his living room. He reached for his .45 automatic and quietly stalked the person sitting in his chair. Not recognizing the young man, he put his hand on his shoulder and asked, "Who in the hell are you, and what are you doing in my chair?"

Waking with a start and seeing the very person he feared most, the young deputy bolted from the chair and out the kitchen door, the screen door slamming in his wake. Sheriff Decker heard the sound of a car motor starting and the squeal of tires in his driveway as he pondered a pair of size 11D patent leather shoes on the floor in front of his easy chair.

As the deputies gathered at the hospital for his final days, they spoke in hushed tones, the occasional subdued chuckle mingled with the moist eyes, and some of the stories of bravery were recaptured.

The deputies all turned and the older ones moved to meet and shake hands with Benny Binion as he entered the hospital waiting room. Lieutenant Wiseman escorted Benny into Decker's hospital room. Decker removed his oxygen mask and sat upright in bed and, for the next few moments, forgot how low sick he was.

Benny said, "Get your close on, Decker, and let's get out of here!"

Decker responded, "I'd like to, Benny, but these damn cigarettes have done me in. I don't have enough power to pull a greased string out of a cat's ass."

Both men laughed and Benny stayed and they reminisced for about fifteen minutes. He would have stayed longer but Decker was fading.

On Saturday, August 29, 1970, in the Lovers Lane Methodist Church, Benny Binion sat wedged into a pew of the church, which was packed and overflowing as over two thousand people were attending Decker's funeral.

Benny was sweating, and tears were flowing freely down his cheeks as Reverend Tom Shipp eulogized Decker from the pulpit.

In April 1971, Benny Binion in Las Vegas got a call from the Reverend Tom Shipp of the Lovers Lane United Methodist Church. They reminisced about how Benny used to sit on the back row while Tom was preaching. Benny would be folding a piece of paper into a paper eagle that he would put in the collection plate. Since he was sitting on the back row, the paper eagle would always be on the top of all the money in the collection plate. The paper eagle was always a one-hundred-dollar bill that Benny had saved for that purpose.

Reverend Shipp got down to business and told Benny that the church was interested in a parcel of land that Benny owned at the intersection of Inwood Road and South West Highway. He asked Benny to come to Dallas to discuss the matter with his committee. Benny responded that he could not come to Dallas and asked Reverend Shipp to come to Las Vegas.

When Reverend Shipp indicated he would not be comfortable in Las Vegas, Binion suggested that they meet halfway in Albuquerque. Later at a breakfast meeting in the Ambassador Hotel, Reverend Shipp was presenting comparable land price sales of contagious properties and finally made Benny what he considered to be a fair price for his six point six acres of land—one hundred and thirty-five thousand dollars.

Benny took a deep pull on his cigar and glared at the group through the smoke as he exhaled and said, "I've decided to sell you that land at the price you have offered!" He broke into laughter when he asked, "Would you like to flip a coin double or nothing?"

The Lovers Lane United Methodist Church stands today at the intersection of Inwood Road and Northwest Highway in Dallas, Texas, six point six acres of land from Benny Binion and three acres from Troy Post.

BENNY'S FINAL GIFT
TO LAS VEGAS

Benny's final gift to Las Vegas was the "World Series Winner-Take-All Poker Game." Other casinos were not interested in offering space to play poker. The return per square foot, generated by the accepted games of dice, blackjack, roulette, and slot machines, was amazing. The other casinos did not want to devote valuable space to what they considered less-profitable poker.

The secret of the success of World Championship Poker was the $10,000 buy-in. Depending on the number of players, for example, twenty-five buy-ins would equal a quarter of a million-dollar pot. The prospects of that kind of money and bragging rights lured the rich, as well as unknown players and prodigies. "Amarillo Slim" Preston and Johnny Moss were among the professionals who hoped to pluck a few of the rich newcomers, and they usually did. But sometimes the new guys had a run of cards and won and, in turn, would become a poker legend themselves.

In order to avoid lengthy games that would bore the spectators, Benny put in place progressive rules that forced the poker game to an early conclusion. World Championship Poker caught the attention of television viewers, and within a few years, tournament poker has gathered national attention.

The Horseshoe has faded into Las Vegas history. It wasn't the classiest joint in Las Vegas, but it had its day. When you met Benny Binion, you knew that you were in the presence of a man who had played a large role in the making of Las Vegas.

At age eighty-five, on Christmas Day 1989, Benny Binion died of congestive heart failure at Valley Hospital in Las Vegas. After a rosary service, he was buried at a cemetery just blocks from his downtown casino.

You could say he was the last one left standing. He had hustled, fought, schemed, and connived to stay ahead of the smartest, meanest, and most treacherous men of his time. Benny Binion has left an indelible imprint on Dallas history and the world of gambling.